Out-of-This-World
Astronomy

Out-of-This-World Astronomy

50 Amazing Activities & Projects

Joe Rhatigan & Rain Newcomb

with Greg Doppmann, Ph.D.,
special consultant

LARK BOOKS

A Division of Sterling Publishing Co., Inc.
New York

SPECIAL CONSULTANT:
Greg Doppmann, Ph.D.

ART DIRECTION & PRODUCTION:
Celia Naranjo

PHOTOGRAPHER:
Steve Mann

COVER DESIGNER:
Barbara Zaretsky

ILLUSTRATOR:
Orrin Lundgren

ASSOCIATE ART DIRECTOR
& PRODUCTION:
Shannon Yokeley

EDITORIAL ASSISTANCE:
Cindy Burda, Delores Gosnell,
Veronika Alice Gunter, and
Nathalie Mornu

EDITORIAL INTERNS:
Robin Heimer and Rebecca Lim

SPECIAL PHOTOGRAPHY:
Robert D. Miller

PROOFREADER:
Jeanée Ledoux

Library of Congress Cataloging-in-Publication Data

Rhatigan, Joe.
   Out-of-this-world astronomy : 50 amazing activities & projects /
Joe Rhatigan & Rain Newcomb.— 1st ed.
       p. cm.
Includes index.
Summary: Introduces "the study of stuff in space," providing statistics,
quizzes, activities, and experiments about the stars and planets.
   ISBN 1-57990-410-6 (hardcover)
   1. Astronomy—Juvenile literature. 2.
Astronomy—Experiments--Juvenile literature. [1. Astronomy. 2.
Astronomy—Experiments. 3. Experiments.] I. Newcomb, Rain. II. Title.
   QB46.R527 2003
   520—dc21

                                                            2003005196

10 9 8 7 6 5 4 3 2 1

First Edition

Published by Lark Books, a division of
Sterling Publishing Co., Inc.
387 Park Avenue South, New York, N.Y. 10016

© 2003, Lark Books

Distributed in Canada by Sterling Publishing,
c/o Canadian Manda Group, One Atlantic Ave., Suite 105
Toronto, Ontario, Canada M6K 3E7

Distributed in the U.K. by Guild of Master Craftsman Publications Ltd.
Castle Place, 166 High Street, Lewes, East Sussex, England
BN7 1XU Tel: (+ 44) 1273 477374, Fax: (+ 44) 1273 478606
Email: pubs@thegmcgroup.com, Web: www.gmcpublications.com

Distributed in Australia by Capricorn Link (Australia) Pty Ltd.
P.O. Box 704, Windsor, NSW 2756 Australia

If you have questions or comments about this book, please contact:
Lark Books
67 Broadway
Asheville, NC 28801
(828) 253-0467

Manufactured in China

1-57990-410-6

*The photograph on page 1 shows
fragments of Comet P/Shoemaker-Levy 9
about to collide with Jupiter.*

Contents

Have you ever looked up
at a starry sky and wondered
if there might be someone far away
who was looking back in your direction,
wondering the same thing?

As a kid, I often wondered about life beyond our special blue planet. One summer, I explored the night sky and became fascinated by views of the Moon, other planets, distant stars, and even colorful nebulae. My imagination was captured, and since then, astronomy has been the ultimate exploration for me, with so many possibilities. Humans have explored almost everything there is to explore here on Earth. So, now, we look to the Universe as our final frontier. And anyone (especially you) who looks up at the sky with curiosity and a desire to know more is an explorer and perhaps a discoverer as well.

As a professional astronomer, I study young stars because I like new beginnings (and birthdays), so I explore how new stars are born. Since my laboratory is the Universe, I simply need to use a big telescope and point it at some stellar nursery. It's fun that I can come to understand something about an object that's so far away from me.

Astronomy is an interesting science in that we study things that are many trillions of miles away. And at this point, we can't get too far into space to find out what's going on out there in person. Sure, we've sent people to the Moon, but the Moon is right in our own backyard. And our farthest-reaching space probe is just now leaving the solar system. (It won't reach another star system for 40,000 years.) But that doesn't mean we can't explore right here from the Earth. In fact, most of what we have learned about our Universe we did by simply looking up at the sky. And what we've observed from our own planet is astonishing.

We've found Pluto, the coldest world of our solar system where gasses are frozen on the surface. We've found out how the nuclear furnace inside the core of our Sun burns and can keep the Sun shining for billions of years. We've located places so far away that you'd have to travel a million, million miles each second just to reach it in your lifetime. We know of such extremes in pressure ranging from the hostile vacuum of space to the cores of neutron stars where atoms themselves are close to being crushed into non-existence. We've seen stars die, and comets crash into planets. We know of colliding galaxies and places where stars are being born right now. We have even detected the very beginnings of the Universe, as it expands outward evermore.

And even before we figure out how to travel to distant worlds, we might find signs of life from the data we collect with our telescopes and space probes. This would be a huge milestone in the history of humankind. In fact, finding out that we are not alone would be bigger than anything else that's ever happened. It is this spirit of exploration and discovery that motivated us to create this book. May it be your stepping stone to understanding more about the Universe and your place within it, whether you want to pursue a career in astronomy like me, or whether you're simply a curious human acquainting yourself with some of your cosmic neighbors in the sky.

Have fun!

— *Greg Doppmann, Ph.D*

"Oooh, What's That?"

It's 35,000 years ago, and you're emerging from your cave, picking mastodon meat from last night's dinner out of your teeth.

You stretch, look up at the sky and...and the big yellow ball in the sky that keeps you warm is disappearing! There's a big bite out of one side of it, and that bite is getting bigger and bigger by the minute. You stand there, frightened to death, yet also unable to run. You know that big yellow ball is a pretty important thing to have, and its disappearance is very alarming. The sky grows dark and you can even see those little dots of light you usually see only at night. You're seriously freaked out. After a few agonizing minutes, you notice the big yellow ball returning. Whew. What a relief. You rush back into your cave dwelling and tell your cave family that a giant mouth in the sky tried to eat the big yellow ball, but the big yellow ball was too hot, so the mouth spit it out.

What!?

Hey, it's not like you and your cave family know what's really going on up there. It will be thousands of years before solar eclipses are understood. (Maybe you guessed that's what you witnessed.) It will be even longer before the telescope is invented and scientists use rockets to explore space. Heck, you don't even have scientists. All you've got is your imagination and a pair of eyes. But that story you told your family is the very beginning of astronomy. You looked up, saw something, and tried to explain it. That's astronomy—the study of anything found in space, whether it's stars, planets, asteroids, black holes, moons, and whatever else we find in the Universe.

We humans have discovered a lot about space since our cave ancestors first studied the sky, and this book will unlock many of the secrets of our fascinating Universe, from our Moon's many faces to our Sun's inner core, from our celestial neighbors in the solar system to the birth and death of stars, and all the way to the outer reaches of the Universe. With tons of activities, projects, and other cool things to do and ponder, *Out-of-This-World Astronomy* will take you on an unforgettable space journey.

What You'll Find Inside

Chapter One will show you how to get started as a sky watcher. You don't need a telescope, and you don't have to know anything at first. All you do is go outside and look up. There's also lots of good information on binoculars and telescopes.

Chapter Two will take you to the Moon, that strange wandering ball that keeps coming and going. Since it's the brightest object in the night sky (most nights), it has been an object of fascination since the dawn of civilization. It's a great place to start your astronomy adventure.

Chapter Three does a fly-by the Sun, which, even though it doesn't come out at night, is a vital clue for astronomers learning about stars and the Universe.

Chapter Four takes you on a guided tour of our space neighborhood—the solar system.

Finally, Chapter Five turns on the warp drive to explore stars that are millions and millions of miles away from us, and how the billions and billions of stars make up millions of millions of galaxies, much like our home galaxy, the Milky Way.

Along the way, we'll dip into the past as well as look into the future. Think about this: We are all in space right now. We are made of the same stuff as those stars that are thousands of light-years away. By attempting to unlock the countless mysteries of the Universe, we're discovering more and more about ourselves and our place in space. We humans are all astronomers searching for the clues, and all you need to do to be a Universe detective is to be fascinated, and imagine.

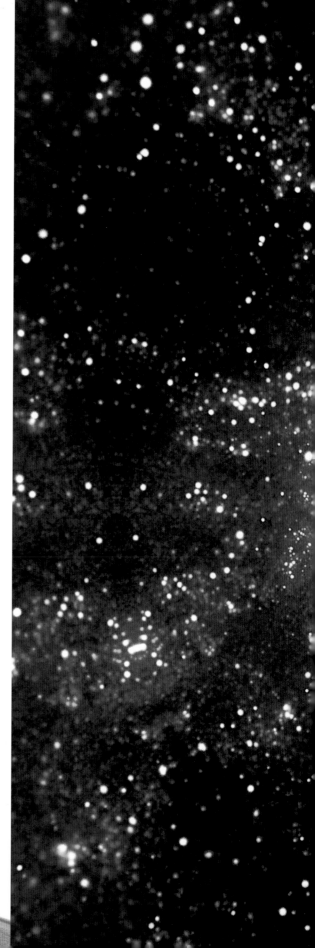

Chapter 1

The View from Here

Sure it's fun looking at cool pictures of stars, planets, asteroids, and more in books, but there's nothing quite like seeing them for real.

Here you'll get all the information you'll need for a front-row seat to observing the sky. It doesn't take much; sometimes all you need are your eyes and a clear, dark night. Just about everything we know about the Universe comes from looking up and staring at the small orbs of light that blanket the sky. And since we can't go to these far-off places (yet!), we usually have to rely on the light we observe to bring us information about all those distant objects.

Stargazer's Notebook

Even before you get outside for your first sky-watching session, take a moment to create a notebook. You can create the one shown here, or simply buy one.

What You Need

○ Computer and printer or ruler, pen, and photocopier
○ 8½ x 11-inch typing paper
○ 3-hole punch
○ 3-ring binder
○ Glow-in-the-dark stickers and other decorative items (optional)

What You Do

1. Create the page (or something like it) below in a word-processing program on the computer. You can also use a ruler and a pen to create one formatted page, and then simply make photocopies.

2. Print a bunch of copies for your book.

3. Use the three-hole punch to make holes in the sheets so they fit in the binder.

4. Decorate the cover of the binder if you want.

5. When you get outside and start observing, write down notes of what you see. In fact, write down every detail you can think of.

Why Take Notes?

Both amateur and professional astronomers like to keep records of their observations not only to note any new discoveries they think they may have found, but also to help them relocate the objects they've observed. Taking notes also helps astronomers look more carefully and notice details they might have missed at first glance. In other words, taking notes makes you look harder and pay more attention.

Date	Time
Location	
Weather	Viewing Instrument Used
Object Observed (if known)	
Details Observed	
Sketch	

Sky Watching

It doesn't matter what night you choose. It doesn't matter what season it is. You don't have to go on an enormous journey to find the darkest spot on Earth. Sky watching is about getting outside at night and seeing for yourself what's up there. Here are some pointers.

Where to Set Up

○ Start out in your backyard or on your porch, deck, or even roof. (Make sure you have a parent's permission and help, of course!) Any open space will do, even if you live in a city.

○ The best time to sky watch is on a clear night with not much moonlight. A spot away from lights and houses is helpful. Too much light makes the sky too bright and blots out most of the stars.

○ If you do live in a big city, or if the moon is full, don't worry. Yes, you'll only see the brightest stars (and perhaps some planets); however, this can make it easier to find major constellations. In other words, if you're just starting out, some light pollution might actually make the sky look less confusing.

What to Bring

○ Telescopes and binoculars are great to have, but you don't need them to enjoy the night sky.

○ When sky watching, you may spend hours sitting or lying outside. Even in the summer, this can make you cold. Don't simply dress for the weather— dress warmer. Wear long-sleeved shirts and pants in the summer (this will also keep bugs away), and wear a hat and gloves in the winter.

○ Wear layers of clothing, so if you're too hot, you can just take some clothes off.

○ If you're going to be sitting on the ground, bring along an old blanket, rug, or other sort of covering to sit or lie on.

○ If you don't want to sit or lie on the ground, bring a reclining lawn chair so your neck won't get sore.

○ Don't forget the snacks. Don't eat greasy chips if you're using a telescope or a pair of binoculars. Bring a thermos of hot chocolate if it's cold out.

○ Get some friends to come with you. Lie down so your heads form a circle. This makes it easier to talk and point things out to each other.

○ Take along your stargazing notebook (see page 12) and a pencil.

○ Finally, bring your trusty, homemade night flashlight (see page 21).

15

Which Way Is Up?

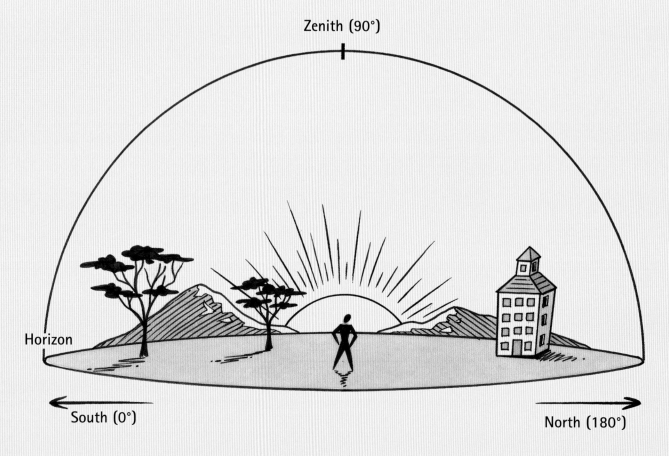

Zenith (90°)

Horizon

South (0°)

North (180°)

For thousands of years, many cultures thought the sky was an upside-down bowl, and if you think about it, who could blame them? Thinking of the sky as a bowl can help you orient yourself to the night sky. Knowing your directions not only helps you find your way in the sky, it also impresses your friends.

❍ Anywhere the "edge" of the bowl touches the ground (where the sky and ground meet) is called the *horizon*.

❍ The spot directly overhead is called the *zenith*.

❍ To find out where north, south, east, and west are, go outside as the Sun is setting. The Sun, and everything in the sky, sets in the west. Why? Because the Earth rotates on its axis once every 24 hours, so the Sun and stars appear to be moving across the sky because *we're* moving.

❍ Once you know where west is, you can figure out the rest. East is

opposite west, so it's directly behind you. South is to your left, and north is to your right. Got it?

❍ The first night you decide to sky watch, go outside as the Sun is setting. Get your bearings. Then go back inside and make your stargazer's notebook and night flashlight. By the time you're through, it'll be dark enough for stargazing.

Flat-Out Wrong!

Ancient cultures spent a lot of time studying the sky.

They also formulated models of what they thought the world and Universe looked like long before anyone could fly out into space and take pictures. In most cases, our ancestors thought our world was flat (it certainly looked flat) with some sort of dome or plate overhead. Here are some examples.

The ancient Chinese believed the sky was a dome or inverted bowl surrounding a flat, square Earth, with the Sun traveling in a tilted circle.

The ancient Egyptians believed that not only was the Earth flat, but so was the sky, which looked a lot like a plate and was kept from crashing to Earth by four gigantic mountains that held it up. What about the Sun? It was carried by boat across the sky. At night it was carried back underground.

The Aztec Indians of Central America believed the world was a flat disk with a great circle of water around it.

The ancient Greeks believed Earth floated in a big ocean-river like a giant cork. Some thought that beyond the sky was a region of fire, which could be seen through holes in the sky. The holes were the Moon, stars, and Sun.

Measuring Distances *in the* Sky

When viewing the sky with friends, it can sometimes be difficult to explain just where a particular star you're looking at is, and it's sort of hard to point up and say, "It's over THERE."

Astronomers think of the sky as half a circle, so they can use the degrees, minutes, and seconds used to measure circles to measure the sky. A full circle is 360 degrees, so the sky from horizon to horizon is 180 degrees. The distance from one horizon to the point directly overhead is 90 degrees (see page 16).

For smaller distances, such as the distance between constellations or stars, use the guidelines that accompany these photos:

An outstretched hand held at arm's length is about 20 degrees wide from the tip of the thumb to the tip of the pinkie—roughly the distance between the first and last stars of the Big Dipper.

If you crook your first finger (pointer finger), the tip of your fingernail to your first knuckle is 2 degrees. From your first knuckle to your second knuckle is 3 degrees, and the second knuckle to the end of your finger is 6 degrees.

A fist at arm's length is about 10 degrees.

A thumb at arm's length is about 2 degrees.

A pinkie at arm's length is 1 degree.

Experiment to see if this works for your hand. The Moon is about half a degree. If your pinkie at arm's length is about 1 degree, then it will be two times wider than the Moon. Finally, you can now direct friends to what you're looking at by first locating a "landmark" you're all familiar with (such as the Big Dipper or other constellation) and using your hand to tell them how many degrees away your observation point is. For example: "It's 15 degrees to the left of the North Star."

Astronomy Clubs & Societies

Don't have a telescope? Don't have a ride out of town? Can't figure out which way to the North Star? There are probably people very near you who are just waiting to help you with any of these astronomical dilemmas. Generally, you can find them in astronomy clubs or societies.

How do you find these clubs? Look at the events section of your local paper. Often, clubs list their meeting times and places in the paper. Is there a planetarium or observatory associated with any of the schools or colleges in your area? Give them a call—they might know where to send you. Try your library—they know about

everything there. If you like using the Internet, search for astronomy societies in your area.

Once you find an astronomy club, get one of your parents (or other responsible adult) to bring you to the first meeting. Sign up for a stargazing field trip or night with the club. You'll have a great time, get to use fancy equipment you could never afford on your allowance, and be surrounded by people who love sky watching. That's really the best part. They know all sorts of stuff about stargazing, and they're probably going to be excited about sharing their knowledge with you.

If you join an astronomy club, you may get a chance to use someone's homemade telescope.

Astronomical Events

Along with the nightly show of stars, the Moon, and planets, there are also astronomical events that happen only at certain times, such as meteor showers, lunar eclipses, conjunctions (when planets line up), comets, and more. You can consult sky maps, newspapers, astronomy websites, and astronomy societies for dates and times of special astronomical events. Mark them on the calendar, gather some friends, and hope for clear skies!

Find out whether or not there is a planetarium or observatory associated with any of the schools in your area.

An Eye Adjustment

When you first get outside at night, you won't see much. Why? Read on.

What You Need

◯ 4 x 6-inch picture frame
◯ Stargazer's notebook and pencil
◯ Watch

What You Do

1. Take the glass, photograph, cardboard insides, and backing out of the picture frame so you're left only with the frame.
2. Wait until nighttime (around 9 p.m. or so), and go outside with the frame. Try to find the darkest place you can. Streetlights and porch lights will make this activity harder to do.
3. Hold the frame up to the Big Dipper or a constellation you're familiar with.
4. Count the stars inside the frame, and write down the number in your notebook.
5. Wait about 10 minutes, hold the frame up to the same spot, and recount the stars you see. Write down the number of stars.
6. Wait another 20 to 30 minutes, and repeat step 5. How many more stars did you see after waiting?

What Just Happened?

When you first go outside at night, you can barely see anything. Your eyes, used to the light from inside your home, can't change quickly enough to see the small amounts of light at night. This is the opposite of someone suddenly turning on a light when you're in a completely dark room. In darkness, the *pupils*, the middle round parts of each eye, slowly dilate or grow bigger to collect more light. The bigger the pupil gets, the more light can enter.

Why do cats see so well at night? Well, have you ever seen how big their pupils get when they're roaming in the dark?

In fact, your eyes are like tiny telescopes with lenses that adjust slowly to the dark to let more light in so you can see fainter and fainter stars. With a telescope, the bigger the primary mirror (the telescope's eye), the more light that can enter. Your eyes will be completely adjusted to the dark after about 30 to 45 minutes, so stick around.

Naked-Eye Sky Watching

Repeat after me: I don't need a telescope to sky watch. Again: I don't need a telescope to sky watch. If you've got one, great; however, you don't need one, especially if astronomy is a brand new hobby for you. Think about it. For thousands of years humans have observed the night sky with nothing more than their eyes. And that's all you need, as well.

What You Can See Using Only Your Eyes

- 2,500 to 3,000 stars and all 88 constellations
- Some of the Moon's craters
- The dark seas of the moon (see page 44)
- Venus, Mercury, Mars, Jupiter, and Saturn
- Star clusters such as the Pleiades in the constellation Taurus
- Gas clouds such as the Great Nebula in the constellation Orion
- The Milky Way winding across the sky
- The great spiral galaxy of Andromeda—the only object that you can see with the naked eye that's outside our home galaxy
- Man-made satellites
- Meteor showers
- The Northern or Southern Lights (Aurora Borealis and the Aurora Australis) if you're close enough to the poles

Astronomy Flashlight

Nothing will ruin your night vision better than the light from a flashlight. Here is a way to avoid this.

If you can find red plastic wrap, wrap a piece over the flashlight, and secure it with a rubber band.

If you have red nail polish, paint it on the glass or plastic cover that's over the light.

The red light from the flashlight won't mess up your night vision, and you'll be able to see your sky-watching notebook and anything else you brought with you. You can even point out stars and other celestial objects with it.

Why Red?

Your eyes are more sensitive to red light than any other color, so you don't need as much of it to be able to see. (This may be why stoplights are red.) When you turn off your red flashlight, your eyes don't need as much time to adjust back to the dark.

Light Pollution

Pollution isn't just the garbage you kindly pick up off the sidewalk. There's also the light pollution we here on Earth create that makes it difficult to see the night sky. Try this activity to see how light pollution affects your view.

This photo is a map of Earth at night. It's pretty easy to tell where most of the world's cities are located. This image was pieced together from several satellite shots of Earth at night. Scientists from the National Aeronautics and Space Administration (NASA) use this map to measure the size of cities and how these cities affect Earth. IMAGE BY CRAIG MAYHEW AND ROBERT SIMMON, NASA GSFC; BASED ON DATA FROM THE DEFENSE METEOROLOGICAL SATELLITE PROGRAM COURTESY OF CHRISTOPHER ELVIDGE, NOAA NATIONAL GEOPHYSICAL DATA CENTER.

What You Need

- ○ A moonless night
- ○ Picture frame from page 20
- ○ Stargazing notebook and a pencil
- ○ Astronomy flashlight (see page 21)

What You Do

1. Before your eyes have adjusted to the dark, find the darkest spot in your backyard.

2. Hold up the picture frame to a familiar constellation or the Big Dipper. Count the stars you see inside the frame and record the number in your notebook.

3. Walk to a site that's not as dark as your first location—perhaps closer to your house. Repeat step 2.

4. Walk to a streetlight or porch light, and repeat step 2.

5. Take a trip into a big city (if you're near one), and repeat step 2.

6. Note how the light here on Earth affected what you could see in the sky.

7. If you want, check your neighborhood to see how people use lights. Are any houses totally illuminated all night? How many lit billboards are there along the roads in your hometown?

What Just Happened?

Light pollution keeps us from being able to see as many stars as we would otherwise see. Light pollution is what happens when artificial lighting is misdirected or overused. Light bounces up into the atmosphere, creating a glow around big cities. This glow makes the light coming from the sky much dimmer and harder to see. Astronomers are finding it increasingly difficult to see the sky, and some observatories located near cities are now more or less useless.

Using Binoculars

Before you ask your parents to raid your college fund to buy a high-powered telescope, consider this: there are amateur astronomers who use nothing but binoculars. A pair of binoculars is essentially two small telescopes strapped together, and a good pair can open up the night sky for you in ways that will blow your mind.

Binocular Tips

❍ When shopping for binoculars, make sure you test them out in the store first. Don't buy the first cheap pair you come across, and remember this: an expensive pair of binoculars will serve you much better than a cheap telescope.

❍ Binoculars are described using a two-number code such as "7 x 35" or "8 x 40." The first number usually ranges from 7 to 10 and refers to the binocular's magnification power. So, if an object is viewed through a 10x binocular, it will appear 10 times larger than if seen with only the naked eye.

❍ The second number refers to the size in millimeters of the second, bigger lenses, called the objective lenses. Most binoculars range from 20 to 60 millimeters. This number determines how much light is captured in an image—the bigger the number, the more light they can collect. And you'll be able to see fainter objects in the sky.

❍ Your binoculars' objective lenses should be at least 35 mm since lenses with smaller diameters don't gather enough light to be much good for sky watching.

❍ For focusing, most binoculars have a central wheel that adjusts both eyepieces at the same time. Some models also have a dial around one of the eyepieces to adjust for a weaker eye.

❍ Don't ever look at the Sun with binoculars!

What You Can See Using Only Binoculars

❍ The star swarm surrounding Orion's belt
❍ The summer Milky Way
❍ Some nebulae
❍ Most of the large craters and mountain ranges of the Moon
❍ Five to 10 times as many stars (plus the stars you observe are steady points of light rather than twinkling)

How to Sky Watch with Binoculars

A great way to observe with binoculars is to sit in a reclining lawn chair. That way you can adjust your position, and you won't get tired standing and staring up. If your chair has arm rests, even better. If you find yourself totally hooked on observing the night sky with binoculars, invest in a camera tripod you can mount the binoculars on. Get a parent to help you with this.

How Binoculars and Telescopes Help Astronomers View the Sky

❍ They make dim objects appear brighter with their light-gathering power.

❍ They make small objects look bigger with their magnification power.

❍ They make clear details on distant or dim objects with their resolution power.

Telescope Power

Ah...the telescope—an astronomer's best friend. Some astronomers love their telescope so much they admit to being just about as fascinated by the instrument as they are by what they can see with it.

Once you've stared at the sky with some friends, and perhaps even scanned the sky with a pair of binoculars, you'll proba- bly want to see what the things you've seen look like through a telescope. Cool. But don't run out and buy the first telescope you find. Read on.

What Exactly Is a Telescope?

In short, any telescope is a "light bucket" that catches as much light as possible in order to make objects in the night sky brighter. Telescopes have another important job as well: to make objects look bigger. Here's how a telescope does both.

THE OBJECTIVE LENS

Every telescope starts with a big lens or mirror called the *objective* that works the same as the one on binoculars. This lens or mirror is designed to catch as much light as possible. The bigger this lens or mirror is, the more light it can catch. And the more light it catches, the brighter it can make dim objects appear. The first important measurement you should know about your telescope is the diameter of the objective. That's called the *aperture*.

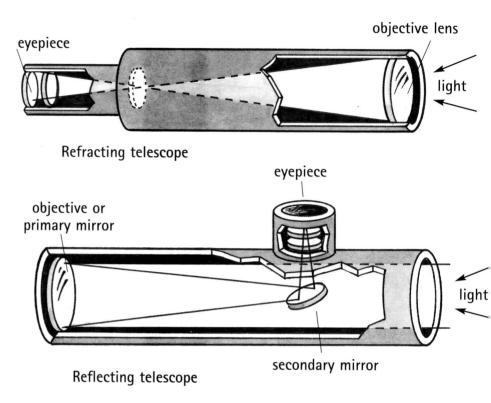

Refracting telescope

Reflecting telescope

THE EYEPIECE

The second stage of the telescope is the *eyepiece*. One way to describe how the eyepiece works is to think of it as acting like a magnifying glass, enlarging the tiny image that the objective lens makes at the focal point. To find the magnification you get with any of your eyepieces, take the focal length of your objective lens and divide it by the focal length of the eyepiece.

Types of Telescopes

The two main types of semiaffordable telescopes are *refractors* and *reflectors*. If your telescope uses a glass lens to collect light, it's called a refractor; if it uses a mirror, it's called a reflector.

REFRACTOR

The refractor telescope is the simple, familiar looking telescope with a long tube. Galileo used one (see page 27). Refractors have two lenses tucked into the tube. The first lens is the objective lens. It gathers the light from whatever it's being pointed at. Then, it bends or *refracts* the light and sends it to the back of the telescope, where the eyepiece is. The eyepiece focuses the light from the objective lens and sends it to your eyes.

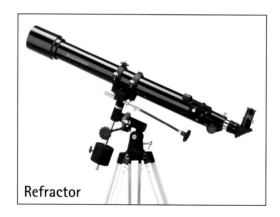

Refractor

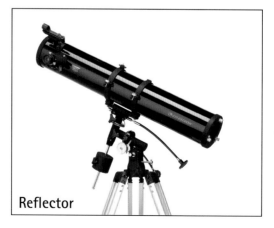

Reflector

REFLECTOR

At one end of the telescope there is a curved mirror, called the primary mirror, which gathers the light from whatever it's pointed at. The primary mirror reflects the image onto the smaller secondary mirror. The secondary mirror reflects the image onto the eyepiece. The eyepiece is the only lens in the telescope. It focuses the light into the viewer's eye. Isaac Newton invented the reflector in 1672.

CATADIOPTRIC

The catadioptric telescope combines the best elements of both the refracting and reflecting telescopes. This telescope is quite

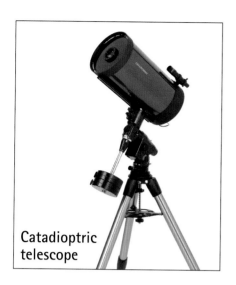

Catadioptric telescope

expensive and is used only by serious amateurs and professional astronomers.

Buying a Telescope

❍ Buy your telescope from a respected dealer rather than at the mall. A dealer will know what she's talking about and can help you find the best telescope in your price range.

❍ Speaking of price range, if you have a limited budget, and you have a choice between an expensive pair of binoculars and a cheap telescope, opt for the binoculars. A cheap telescope will just frustrate you, and it will soon become a clothes hanger in your room.

❍ Buy the telescope with the largest objective lens or mirror you can afford.

❍ A 4-inch-diameter reflector is a good telescope for your money. If you've got big bucks, however, go for the more powerful 8-inch-diameter or even bigger.

❍ A 2$\frac{1}{2}$- to 3-inch-diameter telescope will give you okay power. It's an adequate choice for beginners.

Using Your Telescope

❍ Read and follow the instructions provided by the manufacturer.

❍ Get a chair or stool to sit on or a blanket to kneel on, and a table for your flashlight and books.

❍ Become familiar with the telescope's mount. You'll either have an altazimuth mount, which enables you to move the telescope up and down and/or side to side, or an equatorial mount, which is slightly more sophisticated.

❍ Before you go out to observe a once-in-a-lifetime astronomical event with your brand new telescope, familiarize yourself with the instrument.

❍ Make sure that you have all the parts for your telescope, then set it up inside according to the instructions and put it on its mounting.

❍ If you don't have anything specific to look at, inset the eyepiece with the shortest focal length. This lens will not magnify your image as much as the other lenses, but it lets you look at more stuff at once. After you've found something that intrigues you, put in a different lens.

❍ Center the object you want to look at in the viewfinder. Look through the telescope. If you're not looking at the same object, you'll need to *bore sight* your telescope before you take it out again. (That means you have to align the viewfinder with the main telescope.) In the meantime, pan slowly up and down and across the sky until the object you're looking for pops into your telescope. Lock the mounting's axes and start observing.

❍ Focus the eyepiece of the telescope. To do this, adjust the focusing knob slowly. If the image you're looking at gets bigger or blurrier, start turning the knob the other way. The image you're looking at should focus into a point of light.

Galileo

Galileo Galilei (1564–1642) did not invent the telescope. He did use one, though, and because of it he turned the science of astronomy on its head. He believed the planets orbited the Sun. (Back then this belief was punishable by death.) With his small, 3-inch telescope, he discovered that Jupiter had moons. Galileo observed the Sun through the telescope as well and found all sorts of imperfections on the surface that scientists at the time had no explanation for. (Galileo did look directly at the Sun

through the telescope and it ruined his eyesight.) He also observed the Moon and thought he found vast oceans of water, which even to this day astronomers call "seas."

Why Isn't the Hubble the Biggest Telescope in the World?

The Hubble Space Telescope is 43$\frac{1}{2}$ feet long and 14 feet wide at the biggest point. It's about the size of a tractor-trailer truck. Many telescopes are much bigger than this. But the Hubble doesn't have to be the biggest to be the best. Why? Because it's in orbit around Earth and doesn't have to see through Earth's disruptive atmosphere and light pollution. The Hubble is so accurate it could see a bug flying around your ear from space, and it has photographed nebulae that are 7,000 light-years away (see page 99 for more info on light-years). It has photographed things that are about 4 billion times fainter than anything you can see with just your eyes.

Just a few of the things the Hubble has seen:
- ◯ The birth and death of stars
- ◯ Evidence of massive black holes in the center of galaxies
- ◯ Charon, Pluto's moon
- ◯ Comets crashing into Jupiter
- ◯ Faraway galaxies we never knew existed

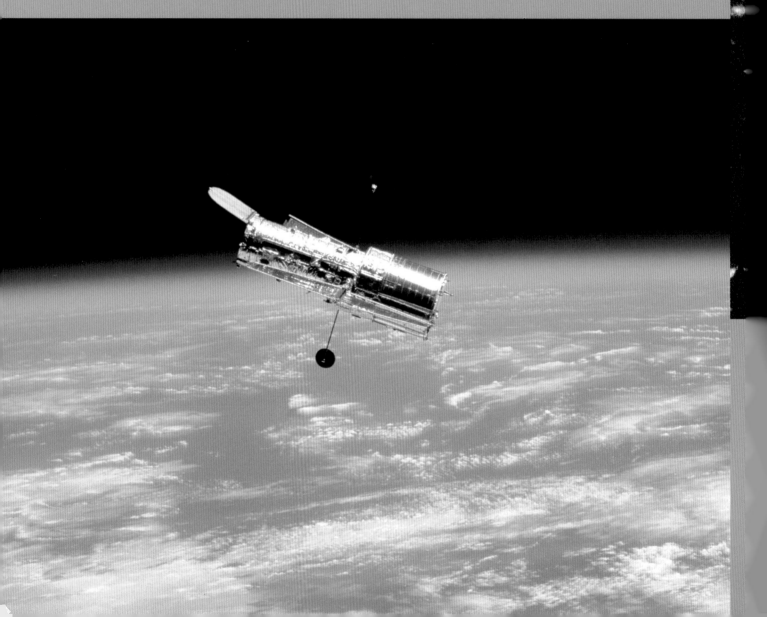

This photograph shows hundreds of galaxies in an area of the sky that is as small as an eye on a coin held at arm's length.

If Bigger Is Better...

Why don't we simply create an enormous telescope the size of Wisconsin and...?

Hold on! Yes, bigger is better when it comes to objective lenses; however, the bigger the mirror or glass, the more likely there are to be flaws in the lens. Also, a glass lens has to be supported from its edges—its weakest part. Mirrors also can become too heavy to support in a telescope. So, we've had to settle for these, the biggest telescopes in the world:

The largest refracting telescope was made in 1897 in Wisconsin, U.S., by a man named George Ellery Hale. His telescope, called the Yerkes Telescope, has a 40-inch objective lens, the tube is 63 feet long, and it weighs 6 tons. It takes another 20 tons of gears to move the telescope. When it was built, it was the largest telescope in the world. It's still used almost every night, and while there are now larger *reflecting* telescopes, this one is still the largest refractor.

The largest reflecting telescope is in Hawaii, U.S., at the Keck Observatory. The primary mirror of this telescope is 400 inches. It weighs about 270 tons. It makes four nanosecond (1,000 times thinner than a piece of your hair) adjustments to the mirror about twice every second. Its light-gathering power is $2^1/_2$ million times the amount your eye can receive.

What's Next?

Plans are underway for the next telescope. So far, it's being called the Next Generation Space Telescope. It will orbit the Sun instead of Earth, have a 26-foot mirror (the Hubble's mirror is 8 feet), and be up to 600 times more sensitive than the Hubble. One of the things astronomers think this new telescope will be able to show them is the mysterious "dark zone"— events that happened in the first billion years after the Big Bang.

Chapter 2

The
Moon

Sometimes you see it; sometimes you don't.

It appears in different shapes and sizes and in different parts of the sky. One night at 9 p.m. it's shining in through your bedroom window. The next night, it's not. You and your friends see a full Moon, and what do you do? You howl at it, just like any other respectable werewolf. When you were a kid you were told of the cow that jumped over the Moon. You may have heard the expression, "The Moon is made of green cheese." And just where is that man in the Moon, anyway? Our closest cousin in the Universe is one strange rock, and it has fueled the human imagination for as long as humans have had imaginations. It's the biggest and brightest light in the night sky. People once told time by the Moon and set up their calendars by it. Some folks used to believe that simply staring at the Moon was enough to drive you insane (the word "lunatic" comes from the Latin name for the Moon, *luna*). Read on to find out what Earth's lone satellite is all about.

Don't forget to howl every now and then!

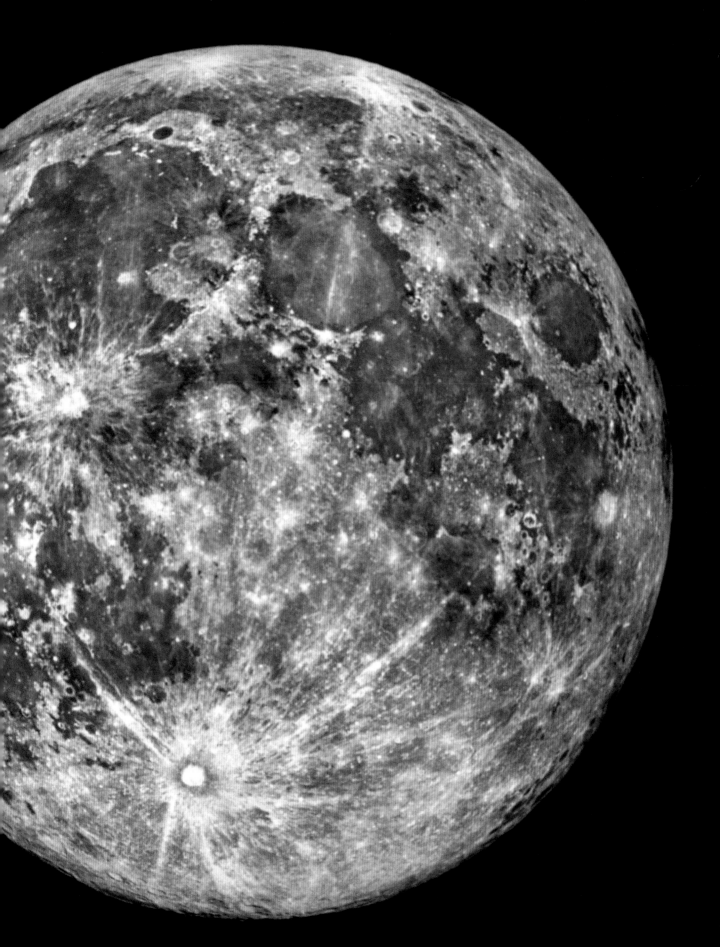

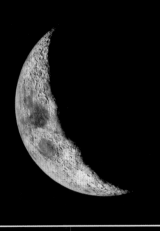

MOON STATS and FACTS

○ The Moon is the fifth-largest moon in the whole solar system.

○ Equatorial diameter: 2,160 miles across

○ Time it takes to rotate once: 29$\frac{1}{2}$ Earth days

○ Time it takes to orbit earth: 29$\frac{1}{2}$ Earth days

○ Length of a lunar year: 1 Earth year

○ Average distance from Earth: 238,000 miles

○ Average surface temperature: from -260°F (dark side) to 240°F (lighted side)

○ Most of the craters on the Moon result from meteor impacts.

○ Atmosphere: none

○ Water: some astronomers think there may be frozen water located at the poles, but nobody knows for sure (yet).

○ The Moon doesn't produce its own light. (Only stars can do that.) It reflects light from the Sun.

○ Moon soil is called *regolith*.

○ There are moonquakes, but they're much less severe than earthquakes.

○ From Earth we always see the same side of the Moon. That's because the amount of time it takes the Moon to rotate once is the same amount of time it takes the Moon to travel around the Earth (see page 40).

○ There are two high tides and two low tides every day on almost every beach on Earth because of the Moon's gravitational pull.

○ Only 12 people have ever walked on the surface of the Moon.

○ Nobody's visited the Moon since 1972.

○ The Moon rises about 40 minutes later on average every night.

○ Much to everyone's chagrin, the Moon is not made out of cheese. It's mostly rock, although it does have a small iron-rich core.

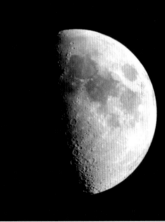
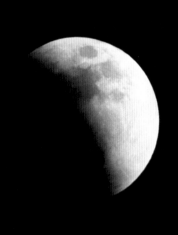

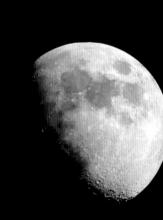

Calculate Your Moon Weight

Sure, you could take your bathroom scale along with you the next time you hitch a ride to the Moon, but it's far easier to figure out your Moon weight using your mind back here on Earth.

What You Need

- ○ Scale
- ○ Paper and pencil
- ○ Calculator
- ○ Chalk
- ○ Stool
- ○ Measuring tape

What You Do

1. Weigh yourself. Write down your weight on the paper.

2. Multiply your weight by .162. For example, if you weigh 80 pounds, multiply .162 by 80. You'd weigh a whopping 13 pounds on the Moon.

3. If you want to know how high you can jump on the Moon, jump as high as you can while standing next to a wall. Have a friend, standing on the stool, mark on the wall how high you jumped. Measure the distance and multiply by six. And the next time someone challenges you to a game of basketball, suggest you play on the Moon.

What Just Happened?

On Earth, when you jump, gravity pulls you back down. Without gravity, you'd just keep going up. Same thing happens on the Moon, except that how strong gravity is depends on how big the planet or moon is and how much *mass* it has. (Mass means the amount of "stuff" the planet or moon is made of.) Since the Moon is so much smaller than Earth, it has much less gravity. In fact, the Moon has only 16.2 percent of the gravity the Earth has. The pull of gravity at the surface of the Moon is so weak, it can't even keep a blanket of gas around the Moon, making it quite difficult for the Moon to develop any sort of atmosphere.

More on Gravity

Hold this book out in front of you. Drop it. Did it fall to the ground? Congratulations, you've just discovered gravity.

Well, not really. People have known about gravity for a very long time. Gravity is a natural force of attraction between any two objects—like this book and the Earth, for example. Sir Isaac Newton (1643-1727) was the first person to really pull together a good theory on gravity. He showed how gravity keeps the Moon orbiting around Earth. Does that seem a little unimpressive? The reason it's so important is that Newton was the first person to say that the way gravity works here on Earth also applies to the way it works in outer space.

Everything has gravity, including you. So why don't little pieces of paper and rocks and stuff orbit around you? Your gravity simply isn't strong enough. The more massive the object is, the more gravity it has. Everything in the Universe is affected by gravity.

Go to the Moon

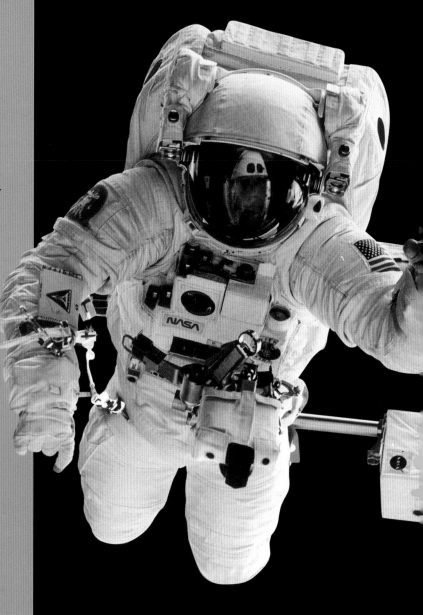

The Moon is the only place in the Universe (except Earth, of course) that humans have visited. Wanna go?

What You Need

○ Space suit
○ Oxygen tanks
○ Water
○ Dried food
○ Camera

What You Do

1. Catch a ride to the Moon. Perhaps some nice astronaut will drop you off on her way to the International Space Station.

2. Suit up! You have to carry your own air with you. The Moon has no atmosphere, hence, no oxygen. Your oxygen, temperature, and humidity controls and communications are in the backpack that came with the space suit. Make sure your suit is strong enough not to tear when you're being pelted by micrometeoroids (you have to dodge the regular-sized meteors). Finally, make sure the visor on your helmet is gold-plated so that most of the Sun's rays are reflected back into space and you aren't instantly blinded and unable to enjoy your trip.

3. Bring along a camera to prove you visited the Moon. Amaze your friends with pictures of the Moon's black sky. The sky is black even when the Sun is shining. Why? No atmosphere. Take shots of the Earth shining in the distance. Make some nasty faces—nobody can see you.

4. See how high you can jump (see page 33). Collect some rocks. Draw something with your foot in the dust. That picture will last millions of years. There's no wind to blow it away. Well, that's about it. Not much else to do. Wait for your ride.

Moon Phases

We all know that the Moon has different phases, but if you thought these phases had something to do with the shadow of the Earth (like many people think), you'd be wrong. Try this activity to see how the Moon's phases really work.

What You Need
○ Basketball or other large ball
○ Permanent marker
○ Desk lamp
○ Dark room

What You Do

1. Place a dot on the ball with the marker. This ball represents the Moon, and since the same side of the Moon always faces the Earth, keep the dot facing you (your head represents Earth).

2. Place the lamp on a table in the middle of the room. Turn it on, and turn off any other lights in the room. The lamp represents (you guessed it) the Sun.

3. Stand several feet away from the light and face it. Hold the ball at arm's length in front of you. If you place the ball directly in front of the light, you just created a solar eclipse. But notice what happens when you place the ball above or below the light. The light strikes the back of the ball and you don't see any light on the side that's facing you. This represents the new Moon phase, which you might as well call the "no Moon" phase since you don't see the Moon at all.

4. Turn a little bit to your left with the ball still at arm's length. You'll notice a small crescent of light on the right side of the ball. This is called the new crescent.

A crescent basketball

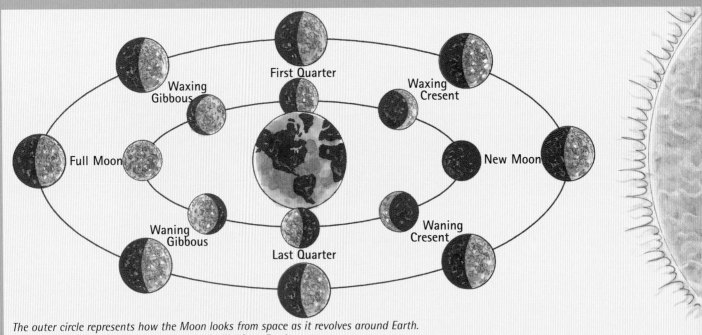
The outer circle represents how the Moon looks from space as it revolves around Earth.
The inner circle shows what the Moon looks like from Earth.

5. Turn until the ball is half lit up. This is called the first quarter Moon. Even though the Moon is half lit, it's called the first quarter since the Moon has traveled one-quarter of the way around the Earth.

First-quarter basketball

6. Continue turning around the circle until you come 180 degrees (halfway around). At this point the whole ball should be lit. It's a full Moon. If your head's in the way, you just created a lunar eclipse. Raise the ball up some to see a full Moon.

7. Continue slowly around the circle until you come back to where you started. Notice along the way the different phases shown on the following page.

What Just Happened?

When the Moon is on the opposite side of Earth from the Sun, the Moon appears fully lit. When the Moon is between the Sun and Earth, it blocks the sunlight and appears dark. During the 29¹/₂ days it takes the Moon to revolve around Earth, it will have different amounts of sunlight striking its surface every day. The amount of sunlight that we see reflected from the Moon's surface during any month is classified into the eight phases.

Find *the* Moon's Phases

Moon Terms to Know
○ The Moon is *waxing* when it's getting bigger and bigger.
○ The Moon is *waning* when it's getting smaller and smaller.
○ *Gibbous* is when the Moon is more than half full, but not completely full. (You can have a waxing or a waning gibbous Moon.)
○ *Crescent* is when the Moon is less than half full, but not completely gone.

New Moon
You can't see this phase. It sets with the Sun.

New (Waxing) Crescent
This phase can be seen just after sunset. It sets soon after.

First Quarter
This half-moon phase rises around midday, when the Sun is already halfway across the sky. It is straight overhead at sunset. It sets around midnight.

Waning crescent

New (Waxing) Gibbous
This almost-full Moon rises after mid-day and sets after midnight.

Full Moon
The full Moon is 180 degrees away from the Sun, so it rises as the Sun sets, and sets as the Sun rises the next day. At midnight, it is straight overhead.

First-quarter

Old (Waning) Gibbous
This phase rises after the Sun sets, and sets after the Sun rises the next day.

Last Quarter
This phase rises around midnight and sets the following day around noon. It's straight overhead at sunrise.

Waxing gibbous

Old (Waning) Crescent
This phase rises sometime after midnight and sets the following day after noon. It's straight overhead at noon, but you won't be able to see it.

Full moon

Lunar Eclipse

What happens during a lunar eclipse is that the Earth gets in between the sun and the Moon. The light that usually shines on the Moon from the sun is blocked by Earth. (You could also say that the Moon is covered by the shadow of the Earth.)

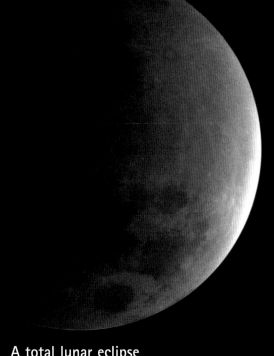

A total lunar eclipse

Types of Lunar Eclipses

A penumbral lunar eclipse isn't very exciting. The Moon passes through the penumbral shadow of the Earth, which is a very faint shadow. If you're watching the Moon closely, you might see a faint dirty gray on the surface of the Moon. But you probably won't.

A partial lunar eclipse is much more interesting. The Moon passes through part of the umbral shadow of the Earth, which is much darker. If you're watching, you'll be able to see the Moon slowly start to disappear. It won't disappear all the way, though, because the Earth and the Moon aren't lined up just right.

A total lunar eclipse is the most spectacular. The Moon passes through the penumbra, the umbra, and then the penumbra again. The entire Moon disappears.

The Moon's orbit is tilted five degrees in relation to Earth's orbit around the Sun. That means it's not orbiting on the same plane as Earth. There are only two points on its orbit where it is lined up with the Earth the right way to have an eclipse. To further complicate matters, the Moon has to be full when it is at one of those two points in order for there to be an eclipse. This happens about once every 8 months.

A partial lunar eclipse

The region of complete shadow is called the umbra. The penumbra is the region of partial shadow, which surrounds the umbra.

If you were on the Moon during a lunar eclipse you would first notice that part of the Sun is blocked off by the Earth, this is when the Moon is in the penumbra of the Earth. When the Moon passes into the umbra of the Earth, it goes into complete shadow and on the Moon you would not see the Sun at all, it would be completely blocked off by Earth.

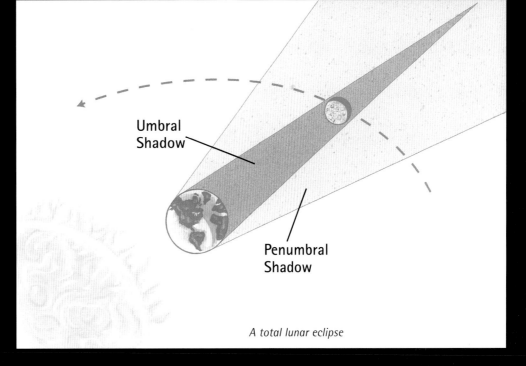

Umbral Shadow

Penumbral Shadow

A total lunar eclipse

Find Your Umbra *and* Penumbra

The shadow of the Earth has two different parts: the umbra and the penumbra. Your shadow does as well.

What You Need
○ A streetlight
○ Nighttime

What You Do

1. Go stand underneath a streetlight at night. Find your shadow.

2. Look at the fuzzy, lighter gray part of your shadow. This is your penumbra. It's bigger than you are, isn't it?

3. Look at the clear, dark part of your shadow. This is your umbra. It's a lot smaller than the penumbra. Is it smaller than you?

The Far Side of the Moon

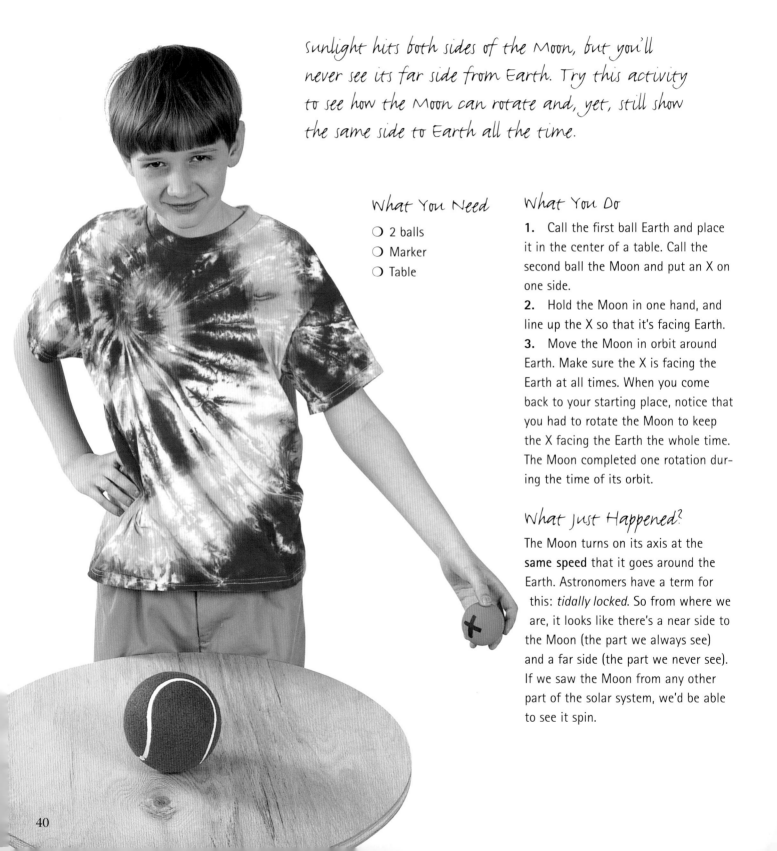

Sunlight hits both sides of the Moon, but you'll never see its far side from Earth. Try this activity to see how the Moon can rotate and, yet, still show the same side to Earth all the time.

What You Need

○ 2 balls
○ Marker
○ Table

What You Do

1.   Call the first ball Earth and place it in the center of a table. Call the second ball the Moon and put an X on one side.

2.   Hold the Moon in one hand, and line up the X so that it's facing Earth.

3.   Move the Moon in orbit around Earth. Make sure the X is facing the Earth at all times. When you come back to your starting place, notice that you had to rotate the Moon to keep the X facing the Earth the whole time. The Moon completed one rotation during the time of its orbit.

What Just Happened?

The Moon turns on its axis at the **same speed** that it goes around the Earth. Astronomers have a term for this: *tidally locked.* So from where we are, it looks like there's a near side to the Moon (the part we always see) and a far side (the part we never see). If we saw the Moon from any other part of the solar system, we'd be able to see it spin.

Do You See What I See?

What do you see when you look at a full Moon?

Is it the famous man in the Moon where the dark areas form his two eyes, nose, and mouth? Or, do you, like people from some Pacific islands, see a woman in the Moon, with the Sea of Tranquility (see page 44) as her hair?

All over the world, people from different cultures see different pictures in the full Moon's light and dark areas. Can you find these pictures in the Moon?
• A woman bent over reading a book
• Crab's claw
• Rabbit
• Toad
• A person carrying a bundle of sticks on his back

What do *you* see?

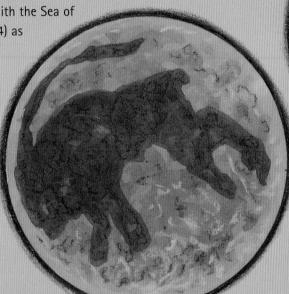

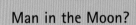
Man in the Moon?

Rabbit in the Moon?

Crab in the Moon?

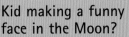
Kid making a funny face in the Moon?

41

Crater Face

If you take a close look at the Moon, you'll notice that it has had a tough time out there in space.

Billions of years ago the Moon, along with every other planet and moon in the solar system, was assaulted by meteors. Re-create the bumpy beginnings of the Moon with this activity.

What You Need

- ○ Old newspaper
- ○ Lasagna pan
- ○ Flour
- ○ Instant hot cocoa mix
- ○ Several small rocks (different sizes)
- ○ Ruler

What You Do

1. Spread the newspaper out on the floor and put the pan on top of it.

2. Fill the pan with 1 to 2 inches of flour.

3. Sprinkle the instant cocoa mix on top of the flour. Try to cover all the flour with a very thin layer of the cocoa.

4. Stand up and drop the smallest rock into the pan. Watch what happens. Remove the rock very carefully and set it aside. Use the ruler to measure how far the flour and cocoa powder flew.

5. Continue to drop rocks into the pan. Drop them from different heights to see how that affects the impact. Take them out of the pan carefully after you've dropped them in.

6. If you're feeling daring, try gently tossing one of the rocks into the pan at an angle. Does that change how the crater looks and how far the debris (the flour and cocoa powder) is flung?

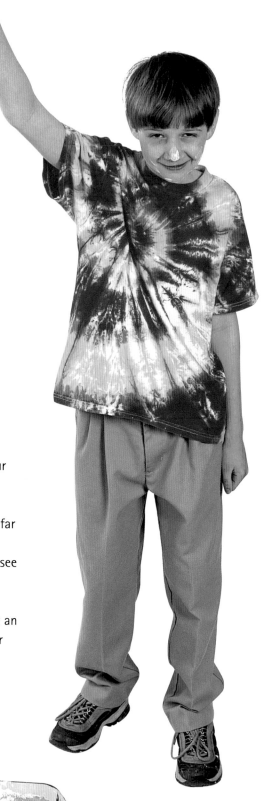

The Barringer Meteor Crater in Arizona, U.S.

What's the Easiest Crater to See with the Naked Eye?

The Barringer Meteor Crater near Winslow, Arizona. It was made 49,000 years ago when a 50-foot meteorite smacked into the desert. Most of the impact craters on Earth have been eroded by the wind and rain. Since the Moon doesn't have either, it still has all of its craters. The easiest crater to see on the Moon with the naked eye is the Tycho crater. Look for it during the gibbous and full phases of the Moon. It's at the bottom edge of the Moon, just a little to the left. You can see the dazzling rays that scatter outward from the crater for hundreds of miles.

What Just Happened?

The craters you made in this activity are similar to the ones on the Moon. Craters are created when meteors, traveling at great speeds, crash into the Moon (see more on meteors on page 94). When they impact and a crater is formed, debris is scattered all over the place. The Moon's surface is covered with craters. Most of them got there about 4.5 billion years ago when the solar system was forming. There was a lot more space junk (like meteors) floating around then, so all the planets and moons were heavily bombarded during that time. Cratering is still happening, just not nearly as frequently as it was then. The two things that determine the size of craters are the size of the meteor and the speed of impact.

One of the Moon's many craters.

Looking *for* Lunar Seas

When Galileo observed the Moon nearly 400 years ago with his telescope, he decided the dark areas on the Moon were seas filled with water. He called them "maria" (Latin for "seas").

What You Need

○ Binoculars or telescope
○ Any night when the Moon isn't full*

*A full Moon is usually too bright for you to see good details.

Sea of Rains
Sea of Cold
Sea of Serenity
Ocean of Storms
Sea of Tranquility
Sea of Crisis
Seething Bay
Sea of Fertility
Sea of Moisture
Sea of Nectar
Sea of Clouds
Central Bay
Sea of Vapors

Sorry, these aren't real seas.

What You Do

1. Get set up outside for some sky watching. Observe the Moon.
2. The first thing you'll probably notice are the light and dark regions on its surface. The light areas are the lunar highlands—usually mountainous terrain covered by craters. The darker areas are the lunar maria.
3. See if you can find the maria noted in the illustration above.

More on Maria

The Moon's maria are dry-land areas created when meteors collided with the Moon 4 billion years ago. These seas *were* filled with something—not water, but lava. Some of the meteor collisions were so forceful, they reached all the way down to the Moon's mantle, which back then was molten lava. The lava flowed to the surface and filled in the crater the meteor made in the first place. Over time the lava cooled into the smooth plains we see today. So, even though there are no real seas on the Moon, that's what they're still called.

The Moon Illusion

Have you ever noticed that the Moon appears to be a whole lot closer to you when it rises?

It's gigantic!

Why does it get smaller when it gets farther up in the sky?

It doesn't, actually. It's an optical illusion that the Moon changes size. It appears bigger when it's closer to the horizon because your eyes can compare it to the things on Earth that are close to it. When it moves higher into the sky, your eyes lose that perspective and then the Moon looks smaller. Don't believe it? Stand on your head and look at the Moon when it's close to the horizon.

If you can't stand on your head, just stick your arm straight out in front of you. Extend your pinkie and measure the Moon with it. Wait until the Moon is well above the horizon and do it again. See? The Moon is the same size.

Mapping *the* Moon:
A 29½–Day Journey

What You Need

○ Binoculars or telescope
○ Stargazer's notebook or a large piece of poster board
○ Colored pencils

What You Do

1. Begin this activity during the first night you can see the Moon after the new Moon phase. Draw what you see.

2. Follow it day by day as the Moon slowly waxes. You'll see how the line of the lunar sunrise gradually reveals the ragged outlines of mountains and craters. This line is called the *terminator*, and it separates the Moon's day and night. The best time to observe and draw the craters on the Moon is when the termina-

tor is intersecting them. When you look at craters on the light half of the Moon, all the sunlight is hitting them at the same angle, so they look flat and shallow. When a crater is intersected by the terminator, you can see the shadows formed by the rim of the crater. This helps you see the three-dimensional parts of the crater.

3. As you get to the full Moon, you'll see all the maria. Check out the long streaks of light emerging from Tycho. You're looking at the splashes of Moon material that sprayed out after the collision.

Did You Know?

Earthshine is the reflection of light from the Sun that bounces off Earth and hits the Moon and lights up its dark part very faintly.

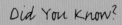

Left Behind *on the* Moon

- A golf ball Alan Shepard hit in 1971
- Astronauts' footprints and tire tracks (They will be there for millions of years since there is no wind or weather to erase them. Maybe they'll get struck by a meteor, but that's a big maybe.)
- Six U.S. flags
- Six plaques
- Four mirrors that can reflect pulses of laser light fired from our planet (These are used to tell how far the Moon is from the Earth, and to find out more about the Moon's rotation and effect on tides.)
- Seismometers (We use them on Earth for measuring earthquakes. On the Moon they record the strength of meteor impacts.)
- A gold olive branch, a traditional symbol of peace, left by Neil Armstrong
- The Lunar Rover and its television camera from Apollo 17 (It took a picture of the crew taking off.)
- Space suits and shoes
- *Streptococcus mitis*, a common bacteria found in the mouth of nearly every human being on Earth. The bacteria went to the Moon accidentally with one of the Surveyor probes. It survived there for nearly three years!

If you want to create something that will last millions of years, leave a footprint on the Moon.

Hey, who left this here?

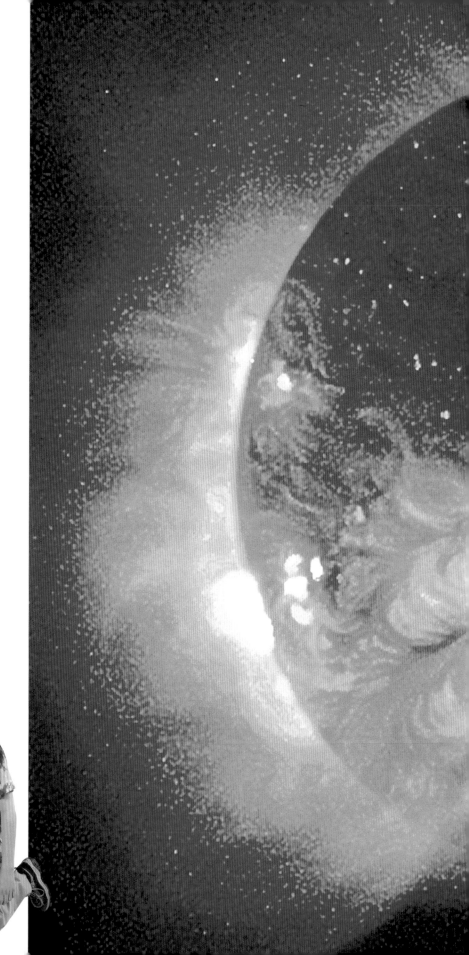

Chapter 3

The Sun

Who says astronomy is only for nighttime?

When you're outside during the day, you'll witness the closest star to us in the whole Universe: the Sun—our very own star only 93 million miles away. Some people may have a hard time believing the Sun is the same as those twinkling dots in the night sky; however, if the Sun were as far away as the rest of the stars, it, too, would be only a twinkling dot in the sky (and not much help to us here on Earth). Sure the Sun looks big, but it's really only an average-sized star called a yellow dwarf. A dwarf? Well, this dwarf is one powerful star. The Sun affects our weather, our food supply, our daily rhythms, and just about everything else we need to survive. Observing the Sun gives us not only clues about life here on Earth, but also clues about the rest of the stars in the Universe.

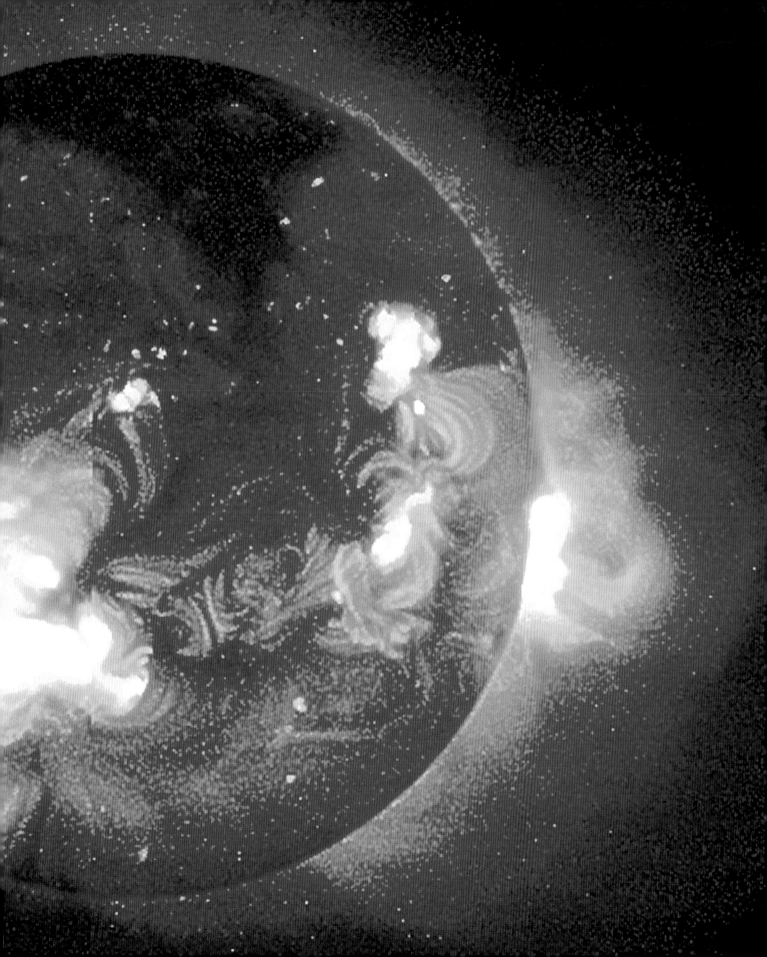

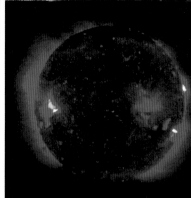

Sun Stats *and* Facts

- ○ Size: 870,000 miles across
- ○ Surface temperature: 10,000° F
- ○ Core temperature: 29 million° F
- ○ Distance from Earth: 93 million miles
- ○ The Sun is a yellow dwarf star, which means it's a pretty average size as far as stars go. This term doesn't mean our Sun is tiny. There are stars that are much, much bigger, and there are stars that are much, much smaller.
- ○ You could fit 109 Earths across the Sun's diameter.
- ○ You could fit nearly 1.3 million Earths inside the whole Sun.
- ○ It takes the Sun's light 8 minutes and 20 seconds to reach the Earth.
- ○ The Sun doesn't spin like a solid ball. At the equator it takes 27 days to make a full rotation. However, near the poles, it takes 34 days to go full circle. This is called *differential rotation.*
- ○ The Sun travels a lot like the planets in our solar system do. The Sun is orbiting around the center of the Milky Way galaxy. It takes about 225 million years to complete one orbit. So, don't hold your breath.
- ○ The Sun is nearly 400,000 times brighter than the full Moon.
- ○ The Earth's atmosphere helps shield us from much of the Sun's harmful radiation.

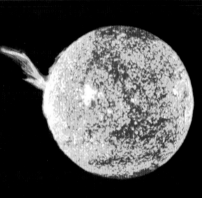

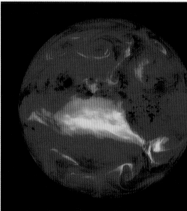

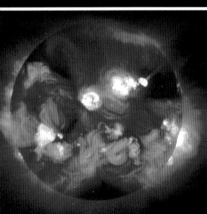

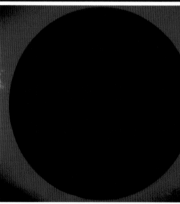

How *the* Sun Works

It isn't easy being a star, shining your light into the Universe, swirling around the galaxy, controlling the orbits of all the planets in the solar system, and awakening any inhabitants of the solar system who happen to be trying to get a little sleep at the wrong time.

How does the Sun do it all? Well, mostly through one simple nuclear reaction. In the center of the Sun, where things are hot and squished together, a nuclear reaction takes place. Two hydrogen protons and two hydrogen neutrons smash and fuse together, turning into helium. In the process, energy is created. This energy works its way up to the surface of the Sun. Between 100,000 and 200,000 years later, the energy reaches the surface of the Sun and is pushed out as light and heat. From there, it takes the light a mere 8 minutes and 20 seconds to reach Earth.

As far as the orbits go, that's a simple matter of gravity. The Moon orbits the Earth because Earth is bigger than the Moon, and the Moon has no choice. The Sun is bigger than anything else in our solar system, so everything orbits around it. Same reason, no choice.

Anatomy of the Sun

The sun is made up of three outer layers. Scientists are sure there's some crazy stuff going on inside the sun, but they can't observe that as easily as they can observe what's happening on the surface.

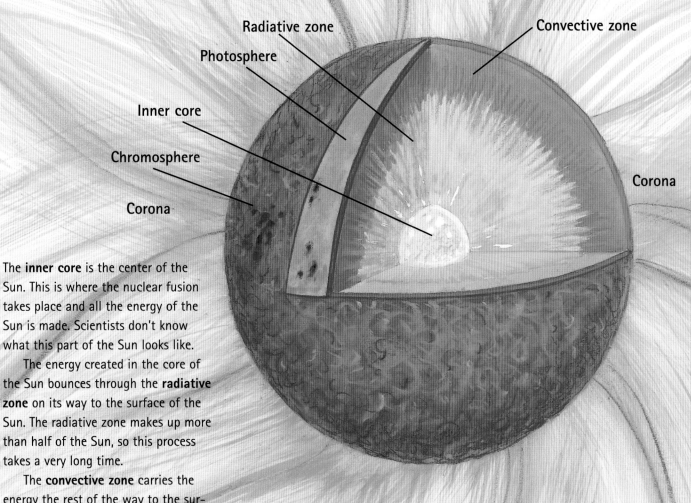

Radiative zone

Photosphere

Inner core

Chromosphere

Corona

Convective zone

Corona

The **inner core** is the center of the Sun. This is where the nuclear fusion takes place and all the energy of the Sun is made. Scientists don't know what this part of the Sun looks like.

The energy created in the core of the Sun bounces through the **radiative zone** on its way to the surface of the Sun. The radiative zone makes up more than half of the Sun, so this process takes a very long time.

The **convective zone** carries the energy the rest of the way to the surface of the Sun. The hot energy rises to the surface of the Sun, cools, and sinks back down. There it warms up and rises again.

The **photosphere** is the surface of the Sun. You couldn't actually stand on it, though, because the Sun is made entirely of gases. The photosphere is the part of the Sun that you can see.

The **chromosphere** is a thick layer of gas just above the photosphere. This part of the Sun can be seen only with a special telescope that filters out all light wavelengths but red light.

The **corona** is the outermost layer of the Sun. It's a very thin, faint layer that's nearly impossible to view from Earth. You can see it in photographs of total solar eclipses. The corona sends out all sorts of energy, including X rays. The corona is millions of degrees hotter than the photosphere, and scientists don't know why.

A Day Trip
to the Sun

Find a big ball (see photo), a pea (see photo), and a long tape measure. This activity will give you some idea of the distance between Earth and the sun, and how they compare in size. Ready to be surprised?

What You Need
○ Big ball
○ Pea
○ Tape measure
○ Pencil and paper
○ Calculator

What You Do

1. The ball represents the Sun, and believe it or not, the pea is Earth. Place the Sun and Earth next to each other on the ground.

2. Measure the circumference of the ball by wrapping the tape measure around the thickest part of the ball (its "equator"). Write down the measurement.

3. To find out the ball's diameter, divide the measurement you wrote down in step 2 by 3.14 (which is pi—if you don't know what pi is, don't worry, trust us for now, and wait until it comes up in math class). For example, say your ball's circumference is 78 inches. Divide 78 inches by 3.14 to get 25 inches. That's the diameter of the ball.

4. Now for the fun. Earth is about 100 Sun diameters away from the Sun. That means you could fit 100 Suns between Earth and the real Sun. So, in order to get the pea (Earth) and the ball (Sun) the correct distance apart, multiply the Sun's diameter (in our example, 25 inches) by 100. In our example that would be 2,500 inches away, which is equal to 208 feet.

5. Measure out the distance you came up with (use the tape measure) along a long, straight sidewalk or field. Have a friend help you.

6. Pick up your pea and start walking. Place the Sun at one end and the Earth on the other end. Want a Moon? Eat three-quarters of another pea, and leave what's left next to the Earth pea.

Sun

Earth

Start walking here!

53

Far Out, *yet* Still Hot

Even at 93 million miles away, the sun's still strong enough to give you one massive sunburn. Make this simple solar oven to see if the sun's hot enough to bake your cookies.

What You Need
- Tape
- Aluminum foil
- Medium-sized pizza box
- Black paper
- Ruler
- Pencil
- Scissors
- Glue
- Cellophane or other clear plastic sheet
- String
- Cookie dough
- Cookie sheet
- Sunny spot

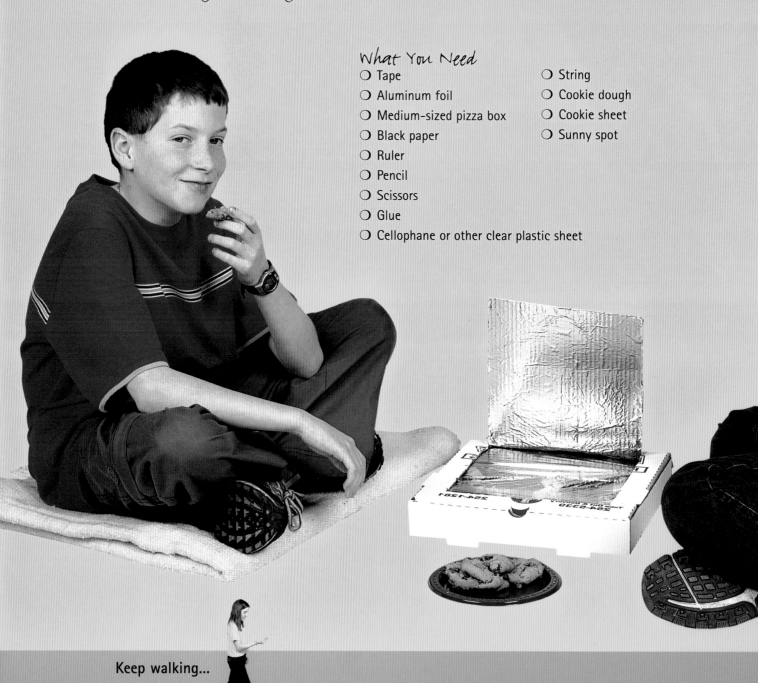

Keep walking...

What You Do

1. Tape the aluminum foil shiny side up to the inside bottom of the pizza box. Cover the foil you just taped to the bottom with black paper. Tape the black paper to the bottom.

2. With the ruler and pencil draw a line 1 inch from all sides of the top of the box. With the scissors, cut the front and side lines, but not the back. (This is the "hinge" for the oven door.) Fold the door open.

3. Cover the inside of the oven door with a piece of aluminum foil. Glue the foil into place. Make sure the shiny side faces into the oven. Smooth out any wrinkles in the foil.

4. Cut a piece of plastic big enough to cover the opening in the pizza lid you cut out in step 2. Tape the plastic piece to one side first, then the opposite side, stretching it tight. Tape the other two sides so no air will get inside the box.

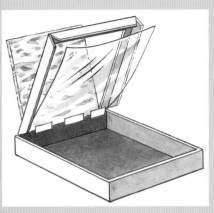

5. Cut a piece of string that will hold the oven door open when cooking. Tape one end of the string to the top of the door, and the other to the back of the pizza box. Adjust the string so the flap stays open.

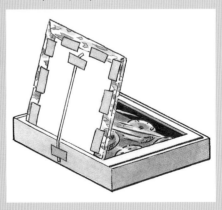

6. Place your cookie dough on a cookie sheet, open the pizza lid, and place the cookies in the solar oven (under the plastic). Find a sunny spot to bake your cookies. Save some for us.

Don't stop   yet...

55

Horizon Calendar

Many ancient cultures used the rising or setting Sun to create calendars. Observe the setting Sun once a week for as long as you can to come up with your own calendar.

What You Need
○ 11 x 17-inch piece of white paper
○ Pencil
○ Clear view of the western horizon (where the Sun sets)
○ Compass
○ Watch

What You Do
1. On the first day of your observation, watch the Sun set, and draw the horizon landmarks at the bottom of the page. The horizon landmarks would be things like trees, houses, streetlights, and the horizon itself. For instance, if the horizon is hilly, you would draw that. Hold your pencil out at arm's length to help you estimate the distances between things.
2. Use the compass to mark west, northwest, and southwest on the page.
3. Note on the horizon picture where the Sun sets. Draw a small sun, and write the date and time inside it.

SW

W

Keep walking...

56

4.   A week later, watch the Sun set from the same location. Mark the spot with the date and time on the horizon drawing you made.

5.   Continue observing the sunset once a week for as long as possible. Add extensions to your piece of paper if you have to.

6.   Look at your horizon calendar and guess where the Sun will set in three days, three months, and six months. Mark these spots on your calendar.

7.   Test your guesses on the days you marked by going outside and watching where the Sun sets. Did it set where you thought it would?

8.   Figure out what time of year it is when the Sun sets at the farthest point on the left side of your paper. What time of year is it when it sets on the right side of your paper? Does the Sun seem to move faster through the sky during some parts of the year?

What Just Happened?

You just observed a phenomenon that people have been observing all over the world for a very long time. Many ancient cultures made horizon calendars so that they could tell what season it was and which one was coming next. They used the calendar to tell them when to plant food, when to move to new camps, and when to hold religious festivals.

NW

...tired yet?...

Equinoxes and Solstices

As the Earth tilts and goes around the Sun, changing the seasons and everything, it reaches four places in its orbit that are so weird, people have obsessed over them for ages.

The equinox is when day and night are exactly the same length. There are two equinoxes every year, one in the spring and one in the fall.

The solstice is when day and night are completely different lengths. The first is the summer solstice. This is the longest day of the year (meaning there's more sunlight than darkness). The second is the winter solstice, which is the shortest day of the year.

We still mark our seasons by these four days. In fact, these dates have been special for thousands of years and have been the basis of many calendars. Stonehenge (a place in England built nearly 5,000 years ago) is a huge calendar. It tracks solstices, eclipses, and the motions of the planets and stars—but you have to know how to read it. (If its makers left instructions, no one has found them yet.)

Almost there...

Sundial

Ancient cultures used the position of the sun as a clock. Egyptians used two flat sticks in a cross shape and called their device a shadow clock. Making your own version is as easy as...well, sticking a pencil in the ground!

6 AM
8 AM
10 AM
12 PM
2 PM
4 PM
6 PM

Not too much farther...

What You Need
- ○ Paper plate
- ○ Ruler
- ○ Just-sharpened pencil
- ○ Protractor
- ○ Watch

What You Do

1. Draw a straight line across the center of the paper plate with the ruler and pencil. Now draw another line perpendicular to the first line so that the two lines make an X.

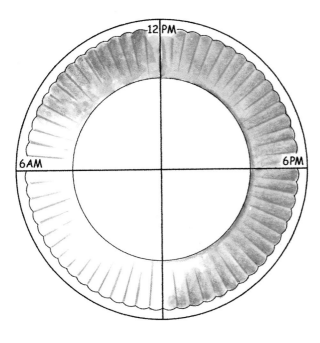

2. Hold the plate so the lines make the shape of a cross. On the left edge of the cross, write "6 a.m." On the top of the cross, write "12 p.m." And on the right side, write "6 p.m." Why aren't you writing anything down on the bottom of the cross? Because the Sun's not out at 12 a.m.

3. Use the protractor to add 15° segments between the hours you wrote down. Write down the missing hours.

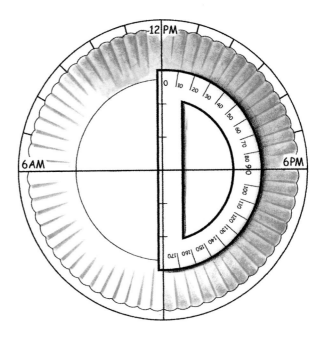

4. Find a sunny, grassy spot outside, and bring the plate and pencil. Place the plate on the grass and carefully poke the pencil through the center of the plate. Push about one-quarter of the pencil into the ground.

5. Turn the plate so the pencil casts a shadow where the hour hand is on your watch. Once that's done, your sundial is ready. Check out the sundial every now and then to see how it's doing. Check it with your watch.

What Just Happened?

The Earth did what it has been doing every day for billions of years. It rotated on its axis. As the Earth spins, sunlight hits it at different angles, so shadows are cast in different directions at different times of the day.

You're here! Your Earth pea has arrived at its orbit, 93 million miles away from the Sun.

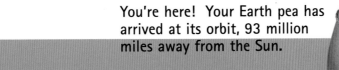

How NOT to View the Sun

Never, ever stare at the sun. Galileo did, and by the end of his life he was quite blind. Even a quick glance can do harm. So, without scaring you any further, here is a good way to "view" a solar eclipse.

What You Need
○ Scissors
○ 2 pieces of white cardboard or stiff paper
○ Tape
○ Aluminum foil
○ Pin
○ A sunny day
○ A friend

What You Do
1. Cut a square out of the center of one of the pieces of cardboard or paper.
2. Tape a piece of aluminum foil over the square hole you just made.
3. Punch a pinhole in the center of the aluminum foil. This is your pinhole camera.
4. Go outside, and place the second piece of cardboard or paper on the ground. Hold the camera up, and aim the hole at the Sun. Remember, don't look at the Sun through the hole.
5. Find the image of the Sun that comes through the hole. Have a friend move the other piece of cardboard until the image rests on the paper and has a nice, crisp edge. What you're seeing is not just a dot of light coming through the hole, but an actual image of the Sun.

Not Viewing *the* Sun *with a* Telescope

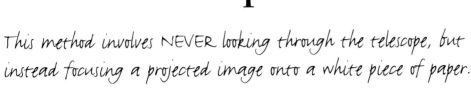

This method involves NEVER looking through the telescope, but instead focusing a projected image onto a white piece of paper.

What You Need

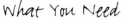

- Telescope mounted on a tripod
- Scissors
- Piece of plain cardboard, at least 12 x 12 inches
- Tape
- Piece of white cardboard or stiff paper, at least 5 x 5 inches
- Strong stick (optional)

Important note: Even if your telescope comes equipped with a Sun filter, don't use it. The only reliable filters are those that fit over the front of the telescope and reflect or block most of the light. Unless you're working alongside an amateur astronomer who knows what he's doing, don't even try looking at the Sun.

What You Do

1. Cut out a small circle in the center of the plain cardboard. Put the cardboard over the front end of the telescope so that light from the small circle you just cut out enters the telescope. Use the tape to secure the cardboard to the telescope if needed. This shades the area where the image of the Sun will appear.

2. Set up the white piece of cardboard behind the telescope. Focus the telescope on infinity by looking at something far away (besides the Sun). Use a low-magnification eyepiece.

3. Point the telescope at the Sun. Adjust the telescope until the Sun appears on the white cardboard. You can align the telescope by moving it until its shadow is as short as possible. There should also be no shadows from the sides of the tube.

4. If the image is fuzzy, move the white cardboard toward or away from the telescope until the image is sharp and clear. The size of the Sun's image can be reduced or enlarged by moving the cardboard in and out, although the telescope will have to be refocused each time you move the cardboard.

Solar Eclipses

When the Moon is in just the right spot between the Earth and the Sun, its shadow blocks out part or all of the Sun, causing a solar eclipse. All eclipses are dangerous to view with the naked eye or any optical equipment. If you're in the right place at the right time, you can use either of the previous two activities to "watch" a solar eclipse.

Three examples of annular eclipses photographed with special equipment.

Solar eclipses happen only at the New Moon. You might guess that eclipses should occur about once a month—but they happen only about twice a year. The Moon's orbit is slightly tilted, so its shadow usually misses our planet during the new Moon.

Types of Solar Eclipses

There are three different types of solar eclipses: *partial*, *total*, and *annular*.

A partial and total solar eclipse take place at the same time. Where you're standing on Earth determines which one you see. In a partial eclipse, the Sun still peeks out from behind the Moon. During a total eclipse, all you can see is the corona of the Sun. (And all the stars that you can't see during the day.) To see a total solar eclipse, you have to be standing in the *Path of Totality*. That's where the darkest part of the Moon's shadow passes over the Earth.

An annular eclipse is a little different. The Moon's orbit around the Earth is elliptical, so it's not a perfect circle. Sometimes it's farther away from the Earth than others. When the Moon is on the far side of its orbit, it's too small to cover the Sun entirely.

Did You Know?

Earth is the only place in the solar system where you can glimpse a total eclipse of the Sun. It doesn't happen on any other planet. By a strange coincidence, the Sun is 900 times bigger than the Moon **and** 900 times farther away, so the Moon and Sun look like they're about the same size from here.

Remember, don't ever look directly at a solar eclipse.

Sun Zits!?

When looking at a projection of the sun (see pages 60 and 61), you may find some dark sunspots on the image. These spots change over a period of several days, and you can track their movement along the surface of the sun.

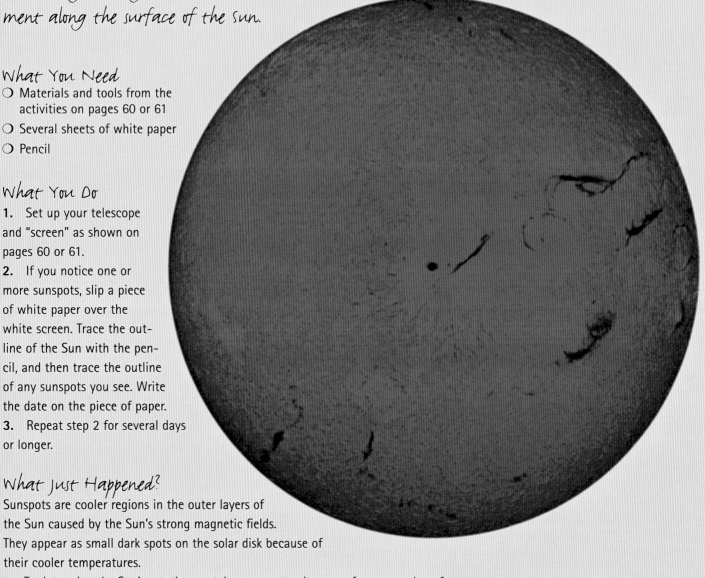

What You Need
○ Materials and tools from the activities on pages 60 or 61
○ Several sheets of white paper
○ Pencil

What You Do
1. Set up your telescope and "screen" as shown on pages 60 or 61.
2. If you notice one or more sunspots, slip a piece of white paper over the white screen. Trace the outline of the Sun with the pencil, and then trace the outline of any sunspots you see. Write the date on the piece of paper.
3. Repeat step 2 for several days or longer.

What Just Happened?
Sunspots are cooler regions in the outer layers of the Sun caused by the Sun's strong magnetic fields. They appear as small dark spots on the solar disk because of their cooler temperatures.

   To determine the Sun's rotation, watch a sunspot as it moves from one edge of the Sun to the other. Because you can see only one side of the Sun, the sunspot has traveled half of the Sun's rotation. Multiply the time it took the sunspots to move across the Sun by two—the sunspots have to travel all the way around the far side of the Sun. You'll probably find that it takes the Sun four weeks or so to make one rotation.

Reasons *for the* Seasons

Ask all the smart people in your life why we have seasons. If any of them say it's because we're either closer or farther away from the sun, tell them they're WRONG. If they think you're just being silly, show them this activity.

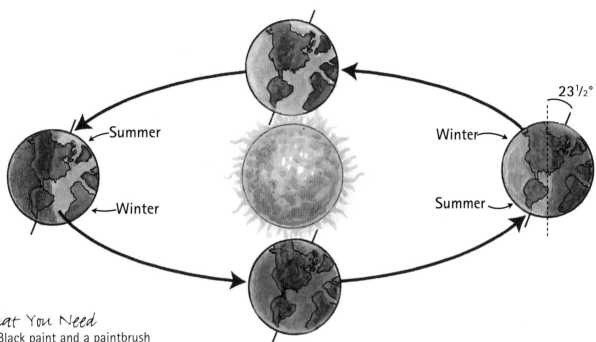

What You Need
- Black paint and a paintbrush
- 2 pieces of cardboard
- Masking tape
- 2 thermometers
- Rocks or bricks to prop up the cardboard

What You Do

1. Paint the two pieces of cardboard black. Once the cardboard pieces are dry, tape one of the thermometers in the center of each piece of cardboard.

2. Place both pieces of cardboard in the shade until the thermometers read the same temperature.

3. Place both pieces of cardboard in the Sun, one propped up by rocks or bricks until the Sun is hitting the thermometer straight on. Lay the second cardboard piece flat on the ground or slightly tilted backward.

4. Check the temperature every couple of minutes. What did you notice? Hmm...seems the piece of cardboard tilted toward the Sun is hotter.

What Just Happened?

The *angle* of the sunlight influences the amount of energy it creates. Light rays hitting straight on are strongest. At an angle, light spreads out and is less intense. This not only explains why it's hotter around noon than it is early in the morning or later in the early evening, but also why it's winter in the northern hemisphere while it's summer in the southern hemisphere. How? Take a look at the illustration above. As Earth rotates, it's tilted about $23\frac{1}{2}$ degrees, instead of being straight up and down like a spinning top. This changes the angle at which sunlight hits the surface as Earth makes its yearly journey around the Sun. The northern hemisphere gets more sunlight when Earth is tipped toward the Sun, so it's hotter (summer). At the same time, the southern hemisphere is tilted away from the Sun. The sunlight spreads out more thinly over a greater area there, so it's colder (winter).

Find Solar Noon

Solar noon is when the sun is at the highest point in the sky, the meridian. Hey, that's easy! Just look at your watch, and when it says noon, the sun will be directly overhead. Well, not quite.

What You Need
○ A sunny day
○ Your local newspaper (today's issue) or a local weather program that tells you the time of the sunrise and sunset for the day
○ Stick
○ Watch, set to the most accurate time possible

What You Do

1. Using your local paper or weather program, figure out the time the Sun rises and sets today. Figure out how much time passes between sunrise and sunset. Divide that number in half. The number you just came up with tells you how long after sunrise the Sun will be at the highest point in the sky.

2. Go outside a little bit before solar noon and stick the stick in a level spot in the ground. When the Sun is at its highest point, the shadow that the stick casts will fall north and south. Look at your watch. It's not noon, is it?

What Just Happened?

Earth does not orbit the Sun at a constant speed. Sure, it always takes us 365.3 days to get all the way around, but some days we travel farther than others. This is because the Sun is slightly off center of the Earth's orbit. When the Earth is closer to the Sun, the Sun's gravity pulls harder on it, so the Earth moves faster. When the Earth is farther away from the Sun, it moves more slowly because the Sun's gravity is not pulling quite so hard.

Rather than creating watches that speed up and slow down depending on where Earth is in its orbit, we use the average speed we travel around the Sun. That is why the Sun will not be at the meridian (the highest point in the sky) each day at noon, except for four days out of the year. The rest of the time the Sun is slightly ahead or slightly behind where it ought to be.

Auroras Explained

Auroras are distinct glowing colors streaked across the night sky, and can be seen with the naked eye.

They are generally best seen at high latitudes near the north or south poles. Sometimes they are seen in places near the equator.

Auroras are caused by the Sun. When sunspots erupt into solar flares, charged particles are flung out, picked up by what's called the solar wind, and carried into the Earth's magnetic field.

Those charged particles filter down through the magnetic field and produce beautiful displays.

You can tell you're seeing an aurora and not a cloud or city lights because you can see the stars shining through the aurora. They usually slowly change in appearance but don't switch directions.

You've probably experienced the

effects that cause an aurora many times and didn't know it. If the reception on your television fades in the middle of your favorite program or if the radio station you're listening to suddenly stops coming in, then it's very possible an aurora might have occurred.

The Northern Lights as seen from space.

Chapter 4

The Solar System

Think about it: A neighborhood where your nearest neighbor (the Moon) is 238,000 miles away.

Our nearest planet neighbor is Venus, which is a mere 26 million miles away. Well, there goes the idea for a neighborhood picnic. Our solar system includes one star, nine orbiting planets, more than 70 moons circling the planets, asteroids, comets, and...well, that's about it. Each planet in our solar system is a unique and fascinating world. They differ in size, surface features, and composition. Each year we seem to get to know our neighbors a little bit better as we send out probes to investigate them. What are we looking for? Perhaps we're looking to understand our home a little bit better and to figure out what things were like when our solar system was much younger. Or, maybe, there are clues to the Universe waiting to be discovered right in our own neighborhood. Let's visit a while.

Solar System Stats *and* Facts

❍ Our solar system is located in the quiet suburbs of the Milky Way galaxy—about 30,000 light-years from the center.

❍ Our solar system, much like the whole Universe, is mostly empty space.

❍ The nine planets in their order of appearance from closest to farthest away are Mercury, Venus, Earth, Mars, Jupiter, Saturn, Uranus, Neptune, and Pluto.

❍ The planets formed around 4.6 billion years ago at the same time as the Sun.

❍ Some astronomers no longer consider Pluto a planet.

❍ Most of the planets orbit the Sun in slightly elliptical paths.

❍ Six of the planets rotate on their axis in a counterclockwise direction. The exceptions are Venus, Uranus, and Pluto.

❍ The planets are broken up into two categories: the terrestrial planets, which include Mercury, Venus, Earth, and Mars; and the Jovian planets, which include Jupiter, Saturn, Uranus, and Neptune.

❍ Pluto doesn't fit either planet category—it's more like an asteroid or the Moon.

❍ Terrestrial planets are located in the inner part of the solar system and are all small, rocky, and dense worlds with solid surfaces.

❍ Jovian planets are located in the outer part of the solar system and are all rapidly rotating, low-density giants with no solid surface.

❍ More than 6,000 large asteroids have been observed in our solar system so far; more than a million asteroids are just over a half-mile wide or smaller.

❍ Some asteroids are so big that some astronomers call them *planetoids*. *Ceres* is the largest of these, and it has a diameter of about 581 miles.

❍ Most of the asteroids in our solar system are located between the orbit of Mars and Jupiter.

❍ Distances in our solar system are often measured in astronomical units (A.U.), which is about 93 million miles (the average distance between Earth and the Sun).

How *the* Solar System Formed: A Theory

The solar system began as a large cloud of interstellar gas and dust.

It was roughly spherical in shape at first. Then the cloud collapsed under its own gravity, getting hotter and denser in the center, spinning and spreading out like a pancake. Eventually, the center of the cloud condensed into the Sun. Meanwhile, the outer parts of the cloud—made up of the lighter, smaller particles of gas and dust—began to run into one another. When the particles collided, they stuck together and got bigger. Things kept running into each other until the particles were as big as the planets and almost all of the interstellar gas and dust was gone. (There's still some of it out at the edges of the solar system.)

The Wanderers

So, what exactly are the planets doing up there?

When humankind first started viewing the sky, they realized that the stars moved around in a big group, their positions in relation to one another not changing at all. (Of course it would be some time before anyone realized that *we* were the ones moving.) It was soon after that our ancestors noticed five "stars" that didn't act like the others. They sort of meandered across the sky in unusual, but predictable, patterns. The ancient Greeks called these five oddballs *planetes*, which means "wanderers." We've since discovered three other wanderers in our solar system, and, though it took some time to figure this out, we now realize that along with Earth, we all orbit around the Sun.

Watching Planets Move

And where in the night sky do you look for a planet?

❍ You can tell a planet from a star by watching it move and looking at its appearance. You'll need several clear, dark nights to watch the inner planets move. Since the outer planets are traveling so much more slowly than the inner ones, you'll need to watch them for weeks, or even years, to see them move.

❍ Once you've found something that you think isn't moving like a star, or twinkling like one, observe the object through a telescope or binoculars. If the object is indeed a star, it will only look brighter. If the object you're looking at is a planet, however, observing it through a telescope or binoculars will show the object to be a disk if the viewing conditions are good enough.

❍ Each planet's movements and appearances are predictable. Astronomy magazines, websites, and star and planet locators provide charts that tell you what planets you can see each day, and when and where you can see them.

❍ The stars circle the sky together, keeping their positions, while the planets move across the star patterns (called constellations). The band of constellations the planets follow are known as the zodiac, and they are Aries, Taurus, Gemini, Cancer, Leo, Virgo, Libra, Scorpio, Sagittarius, Capricorn, Aquarius, and Pisces.

❍ Over time, each planet moves at its own speed from one constellation to another, changing its position in the sky compared to the stars and to the other planets. On any given night a particular planet may be visible lower or higher in the sky, all night or part of the night, or not at all.

❍ The farther away a planet is from us, the more slowly it appears to move against the stars at any time.

❍ Sometimes, as you watch a planet over a period of months, you may see the planet, which had been moving eastward in the sky, suddenly moving backward or westward. What's going on? The planet is being overtaken by Earth. In other words, Earth is moving faster than the planet and has passed it, much like when you're in a car and your car passes another car on the highway. As you pass the slower car, it looks like it's slowing down, and then moving backward. After you pass it, it looks like it's moving forward again. This is called *retrograde motion*.

72

Finding Mercury

You don't need a telescope to observe Mercury, but you have to time your viewing perfectly.

Helpful Hints:

○ Mercury can be viewed sometimes in the evening just after sunset in the west, or sometimes in the early morning just before sunrise in the east.

○ Mercury can be seen with the naked eye, but it is helpful to have binoculars.

○ The best place to view Mercury is at the beach, on a hill, or in a clear field.

○ There are many amateur astronomers who have never even bothered observing Mercury. Why? Mercury moves very quickly through the sky, and it is never more than 28 degrees from the Sun (see page 18 for measuring objects in the sky). That means you can view Mercury only right after the Sun sets or rises (depending on the time of year).

○ If you know where and when to look (check out websites or astronomy magazines), it's an easy planet to spot, either low in the west after the Sun has gone down or in the east at dawn.

○ You can see Mercury's phases with a small telescope.

○ Since Mercury will be visible only very close to the horizon, obstacles such as buildings can get in the way. Plus, our atmosphere along with light pollution can make it difficult to get a clear view of the planet. Choose a place with a dark, unobstructed horizon to view Mercury, and you'll see how moonlike it looks.

○ The later Mercury sets in the evening, the easier it is to see (and it stays around for longer). And, the earlier it rises in the morning, the easier it is to see (it stays around for longer then, too).

Finding Venus

Venus is the easiest planet to spot. If you see an especially bright "star" in the west just after sunset or in the east just before sunrise, it's actually Venus.

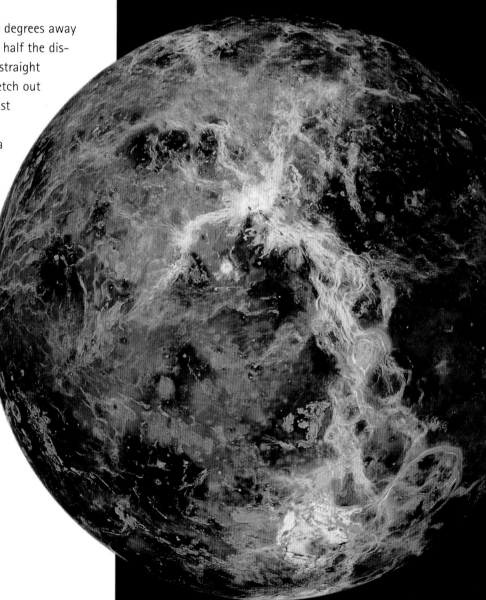

Helpful Hints:

○ Venus appears as a morning "star" for about 263 days. Then, Venus hides behind the Sun for 50 days. When it reappears, it becomes the evening star for about 263 days. Venus is also not visible when it goes in front of the sun for about 8 days. The entire cycle is 584 days long.

○ Venus, like Mercury, undergoes phases, which you can see with a telescope.

○ Venus ranges up to 48 degrees away from the Sun. That's about half the distance from the horizon to straight overhead. (Make a fist, stretch out your arm, and count 4½ fist lengths from the horizon.)

○ Watching Venus over a period of weeks, you see it start off close to the Sun early one evening, and with each passing week, it will look as if it's running away from the Sun. Then it will seem to get tired and slow down. For a few days it will move very slowly, and eventually it will appear to stop moving entirely. Finally it will start moving closer and closer to the Sun until you can't see it for a while.

Finding Mars

Mars is another easy planet to find without a telescope or binoculars.

Helpful Hints:

○ Mars is viewed as a distinct, reddish object, and is more prominent in some years than others. Consult a current astronomy magazine.

○ Since Mars is farther from the Sun than Earth is, it can appear anywhere in the sky. It doesn't stay close to the Sun like the inner planets do.

○ When closest to Earth, it can be a mere 38 million miles from us and twice as bright as Sirius, the brightest star. At other times, the eccentricity of its orbit may place it about 250 million miles away. This far from Earth it looks tiny even through small telescopes.

○ Using a telescope you may be able to see Mars's polar caps grow or shrink as seasons change.

○ Using a telescope you may also be able to see the dark surface features in its southern hemisphere.

○ In the northern hemisphere, you may see Mare Acidalium.

○ If you don't see any details on Mars, there might be a dust storm brewing.

Finding Jupiter

You can see Jupiter without a telescope or binoculars, though with either, you can see its Great Red Spot and its complicated wind patterns.

Helpful Hints:

◯ Jupiter can be the third brightest object in the sky following Venus and the Moon. The planet is so large that, with a pair of binoculars, you can see its color and some of the moons that orbit it.

◯ Along with its Great Red Spot, you can observe Jupiter's cloud patterns, which vary from year to year.

◯ With a small telescope or strong pair of binoculars, you can view the four big moons that Galileo first observed in the 17th century.

◯ The four moons can often be seen passing in front of Jupiter, into Jupiter's shadow, or behind it. If you watch one of the moons for a few minutes, you'll even see it move.

◯ The surface features of Jupiter change constantly as the planet rotates. Be patient.

Finding Saturn

Saturn is the last of the ancient planets that can be seen without aid of a telescope or pair of binoculars.

Helpful Hints:

❍ Saturn appears bright in the night sky. You'll need a telescope or a good pair of binoculars, though, to get a really good view of its famous rings.

❍ Saturn stands out in the night sky because of its brightness and green color. It will look yellow in the northeast after dusk.

❍ With a small telescope you can see Saturn's moon Titan and at least three other moons.

Finding Uranus

Uranus is barely viewable with the naked eye, though you can find it with a pair of binoculars.

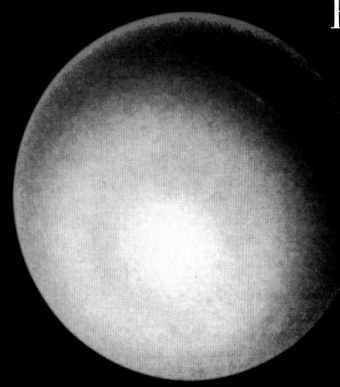

Helpful Hints:

❍ Definitely consult a planet locator or a website so you can find out where Uranus will be in the sky. You probably won't find it just scanning the sky.

❍ Through a telescope Uranus appears as a greenish blue disk.

❍ You won't see any details of the planet, even with a semipowerful telescope.

Finding Neptune

Good luck. Neptune is a challenge to find even on the perfect night with powerful equipment. But if you know what you're doing and where Neptune is supposed to be, you could see it on a very clear night with a good pair of binoculars.

Helpful Hints:

○ You'll need accurate details of its position and good charts from a current astronomy magazine to even attempt to find Neptune.

○ It's hard to pick out Neptune from the faint stars in the sky, so you may want to ask an amateur astronomer to help you find it.

Finding Pluto

Pluto is just about impossible for a beginner astronomer to find.

Helpful Hints:

○ You may get a glimpse of Pluto if you have an 8-inch telescope and if you know exactly where to look. Even then, Pluto is almost impossible to see amidst the stars. Without special equipment to correct distortions, even the most powerful telescope can't see Pluto in any detail. It just looks like a star.

Planet Chart

	Distance from Sun (in miles)	Time it takes to orbit Sun (in Earth time)	Time it takes to rotate once on axis (in Earth time)	Diameter of equator (in miles)	Atmosphere
Mercury	36 million	88 days	59 days	3,000	Virtually none
Venus	65 million	225 days	243 days	7,200	Mostly carbon dioxide
Earth	93 million (1 A.U.)	365.3 days	24 hours	8,000	Mostly nitrogen and oxygen
Mars	142 million	687 days	24 hours, 37 minutes	4,200	Thin layer of carbon dioxide
Jupiter	484 million	11.86 years	10 hours	88,846	Mostly hydrogen, plus some helium
Saturn	885 million	29.46 years	9.8 hours	74,600	Mostly hydrogen, plus some helium
Uranus	1.7 billion	84 years	17 hours	31,570	Mostly hydrogen, with helium and methane
Neptune	2.7 billion	165 years	16 hours, 17 minutes	30,200	Hydrogen, helium, methane
Pluto	3.6 billion	248 years	6 days, 19 hours	1,900	Methane

Moons	Rings	Temperature	When discovered	Name's origin
0	0	-200°F to 800°F	First observed thousands of years ago	Ancient Roman god of travel and thievery; received this name because it moves so quickly across the sky
0	0	900°F	Observed since prehistoric times	Roman goddess of love and beauty; named because it's the brightest planet
1	0	-126°F to 136°F	In the 16th century, Polish astronomer Nicolaus Copernicus realized Earth was just another planet.	From the Old English *eorthe*, meaning ground, firm, or solid
2	0	-191°F to 24°F	Observed since prehistoric times	Roman god of war; named for its blood-red color
17	3	-236°F	Observed since prehistoric times	Roman king of the gods; given the name because of its enormous size
18 or more	7	-285°F	Observed since prehistoric times	Roman god of agriculture
15	11	-357°F	Discovered in 1781 by Sir William Herschel	Roman god of the sky
8	4	-360°F	Discovered in 1846 by astronomers Galle and d'Arrest	Roman god of the sea
1	0	-370°F	Discovered in 1930 by Clyde Tombaugh	Roman god of the underworld; the name was suggested by a schoolgirl

All *about* Earth

Remember the story of Goldilocks and the three bears? Goldilocks breaks into the bears' home and checks out their food, chairs, and beds. She finds the father's stuff too hot, big, or hard; the mother's stuff is too cold, big, or soft; but the kid bear's stuff is just right. Well, some scientists use this story to help explain why there's life on Earth but not on the other planets. How? Take a look.

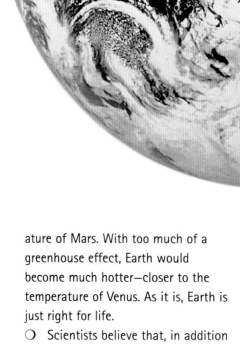

○ According to the Goldilocks Principle, if Earth were any closer to the Sun, it would be too hot for life as we know it. If Earth were any farther away from the Sun, it would be too cold for life.

○ Carbon dioxide, the stuff that you and every other animal on the planet exhales, is an important greenhouse gas. It traps heat from the Sun in the atmosphere, keeping the Earth warm enough to support life. Here on Earth, we have just the right amount of greenhouse gases to keep the Earth at the right temperature for life to exist. Without the greenhouse effect, Earth would be colder—closer to the temper-ature of Mars. With too much of a greenhouse effect, Earth would become much hotter—closer to the temperature of Venus. As it is, Earth is just right for life.

○ Scientists believe that, in addition to an atmosphere like ours, planets also need large amounts of a liquid in order for life to exist there. For us, that liquid is water. In order for the liquid water to exist, the planet has to be just the right distance from its star. Venus is too close to the Sun, so all of its water has boiled off. Mars is too far away, so all of its water is frozen. A small change in the distance of the Earth from the Sun would have a dras-tic effect of its ability to support life.

The Planet Quiz

1. Which planet is known as the morning star?

2. Which planet has liquid water on it?

3. How big are the objects that make up Saturn's rings?

4. Which planet has the largest crater in the solar system?

5. Which moon has liquid water on it?

6. Which planet spins on its side?

7. Why is Venus so bright?

8. What kind of water does Mars have?

9. Where's the coldest spot in the solar system?

10. Which planets spin clockwise?

11. Which planet could you float in a bathtub?

12. What hangs out between Mars and Jupiter?

13. Which planet is farthest from the Sun?

14. Where is the Great Red Spot?

15. Which planets have no moons?

16. Why is Mars red?

17. Which planet is not always considered a planet?

18. Where's the largest volcano in the solar system?

19. Which is the heaviest planet?

20. Which planet has a moon that is almost its same size?

21. Which planet is considered the windiest?

Answers to the Planet Quiz

1. Venus.

2. Earth.

3. They vary in size from a grain of sugar to a house.

4. Mercury. The Caloris Basin is 830 miles wide.

5. Europa, one of Jupiter's moons.

6. Uranus.

7. It's covered in clouds.

8. Frozen water at the poles. If it all melted, the surface of Mars would be 100 feet under water.

9. Triton, one of Neptune's moons, gets down to –391°F!

10. Venus, Uranus, and Pluto.

11. Saturn. But where would you find a bathtub big enough?

12. The asteroid belt.

13. Usually Pluto, although its orbit crosses Neptune's every 238 years, making Neptune the farthest planet out. This will happen next in 2226.

14. On Jupiter. It's a big wind storm.

15. Mercury and Venus.

16. The surface of Mars is covered in rust.

17. Pluto. Some scientists think it's really more of a large asteroid than a small planet.

18. On Mars. Olympus Mons would take up the entire state of Arizona and is more than 17 miles high. (Mount Everest here on Earth is only 5 miles high.)

19. Jupiter. It weighs more than all of the other planets put together.

20. Pluto.

21. Neptune. It has wind gusts up to 1,200 miles per hour.

Traveling Round *the* Sun

Our path around the sun is elliptical rather than a perfect circle. An ellipse is a circle that looks as if it has been slightly flattened. This activity shows what an elliptical orbit looks like, and begins to explain why the planets travel this way.

What You Need
○ Tape
○ Typing paper
○ Piece of corrugated cardboard
○ 2 pushpins
○ Piece of string about 1 foot long
○ Pencil

What You Do

1. Tape the paper to the cardboard.
2. Stick the two pushpins into the center of the paper about 3 inches apart.
3. Tie the ends of the string together to form a loop.
4. Loop the string over the two pushpins.
5. Using the tip of the pencil, form a triangle with the string, keeping it tight.
6. Draw your ellipse with the pencil, keeping the string tight the whole time you're drawing.
7. Remove the pins and string. Each hole is called the ellipse's focus. One of them is the Sun.
8. Draw a planet on the ellipse you made in step 6.
9. Along the planet's orbit, find the place where the planet is closest to the "Sun." This spot is called the planet's *perihelion*. The point farthest from the Sun is called the *aphelion*.

What Just Happened?

Sir Isaac Newton is the scientist who figured out that gravity is the force of attraction between two objects due to their mass (the amount of stuff in an object). It's gravity that keeps the planets orbiting the Sun. No Sun, no elliptical orbit—we'd all be traveling in a straight line. Planets travel faster when they're closer to the Sun because gravity pulls harder on the planet than when it's farther away.

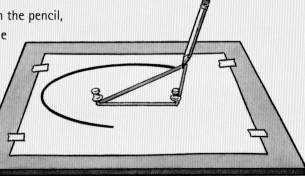

Mercury, Venus, Earth, Mars, Jupiter, Saturn, George, Neptune, Pluto

George!?

That's right. If it were up to William Herschel, the man who discovered Uranus in 1781, it would have been named *Georgium Sidus*, which is Latin for "George's Star." When Herschel made his huge discovery, he wanted to thank his boss, King George the Third of England for his support by naming the planet after him. Hey, it's not like there was a rule that you HAD to name new planets after Roman gods. Astronomers and others, however, still thought it more appropriate to use a mythological name to fit in with the rest of the planets. Uranus (the name of the Roman god of the sky) was finally agreed upon.

Question: Which of the nine planets is not named after a Greek or Roman god?

Answer: Earth (the name Earth is Germanic and Old English in origin).

So who's in charge of naming solar system objects that are discovered now? The International Astronomical Union (IAU) has been in charge of naming all celestial objects. If you find a new planet (or a comet, asteroid, and so on), you can suggest a name to the IAU, but they may or may not accept it.

How Old Are You Now?

Your birthday is actually a celebration of the Earth traveling one complete revolution around the Sun. How old would you be on other planets?

What You Need
○ Calculator
○ Pencil and paper

What You Do

1. Multiply your age by 365 (the number of days in a year).
2. Add the number of days it's been since your last birthday. This is how many days old you are.
3. Divide your age in days by how many Earth days it takes the different planets to go around the Sun. Use the chart provided below.
4. For example, if you're 10 years old, multiply 10 by 365 to get 3,650. Say your birthday was 100 days ago. Add 100 days to 3,650 to get 3,750. If you want to know how old you are on Mars, divide 3,750 by 687 (see chart). Congratulations! You're almost 5½ years old on Mars. Hey, it could be worse. If you were on Jupiter, you wouldn't even be 1 year old yet.

PLANET	DAYS IT TAKES TO GO AROUND SUN
Mercury	88
Venus	225
Earth	365
Mars	687
Jupiter	4,332
Saturn	10,760
Uranus	30,681
Neptune	60,193
Pluto	90,472

A Weighty Matter

Planets that have more mass than the Earth have more gravity, which means things would weigh more on that planet. Check out this phenomenon with this activity.

What You Need

- ○ 9 containers with lids
- ○ Masking tape
- ○ Marker
- ○ 822 pennies
- ○ Relative weight chart (see below)
- ○ Calculator (optional)

What You Do

1. Wash out and dry the containers.
2. With the tape and marker, assign a planet to each container. Don't forget Earth.
3. Place 100 pennies in Earth. This can represent 100 pounds on Earth.

4. Follow the chart below for the rest.
5. Pick up the Earth container that represents 100 pounds, and experience what 100 pounds would feel like on Jupiter by picking up the Jupiter container with your other hand. Do this with each of the planets.
6. To find out how much you weigh on other planets, multiply the relative weight of the planets by your weight. Use a calculator if you want.

What Just Happened?

In the chart, any planet with a number less than Earth's (Mercury, Venus, Mars, Saturn, Uranus, and Pluto) has less gravity than our home planet since it contains less mass than Earth. The remaining planets, Jupiter and Neptune, have more mass than Earth, so they exert a stronger gravitational pull on objects, which is why you weigh more.

Note: A large gaseous planet that isn't very dense may have less surface gravity than a much smaller but denser planet.

PLANET	RELATIVE WEIGHT TO EARTH'S	# PENNIES
Mercury	.38	38
Venus	.91	91
Earth	1.00	100
Mars	.38	38
Jupiter	2.36	236
Saturn	1.05	105
Uranus	.94	94
Neptune	1.13	113
Pluto	.07	7

Football Field Solar System

There are several fun ways to try to get a handle on just how big our solar system is, how far apart the planets are from each other, and just how much empty space there is out there. Here you'll create a scale model solar system using a football field.

What You Need
- ○ Use of a football field
- ○ 10 index cards
- ○ Markers
- ○ Tape
- ○ 10 stakes

What You Do

1. In order to do this activity we have to scale down the solar system until it fits onto our football field. This scaling-down process is similar to what mapmakers do to make things fit onto the piece of paper they're drawing their maps on. For this example 1 A.U. (recall that 1 A.U. is the average distance between the Earth and Sun) equals 3 yards.

2. Write the names of the planets on index cards. Include one with the word "Sun" written on it as well.

3. Tape the index cards to the stakes.

4. Head out to the football field. For this activity, we used a 100-yard football field with 10-yard end zones.

5. Using the chart on page 90, we figured that if we made 1 A.U. equal to 3 yards, the solar system would just about fit on the field. This means that for every 3 yards you travel on the field, you're actually traveling 93 million miles.

6. Place the Sun on the 0 yard line on one end of the field.

7. Place Mercury on the 1 yard line; Venus, 2 yard line; Earth, 3 yard line; Mars, 4½ yard line; Jupiter, 15½ yard line; Saturn, 29 yard line.

8. Uranus is past center field (the 50 yard line) on the 42 yard line (not the first 42 yard line you cross, but the second). Place Neptune on the 10 yard line. And Pluto? Pluto is 18 yards past the 0 yard line. End zones are usually 10 yards deep, so go past the end zone and measure an extra 8 yards (21 feet). That's where Pluto goes.

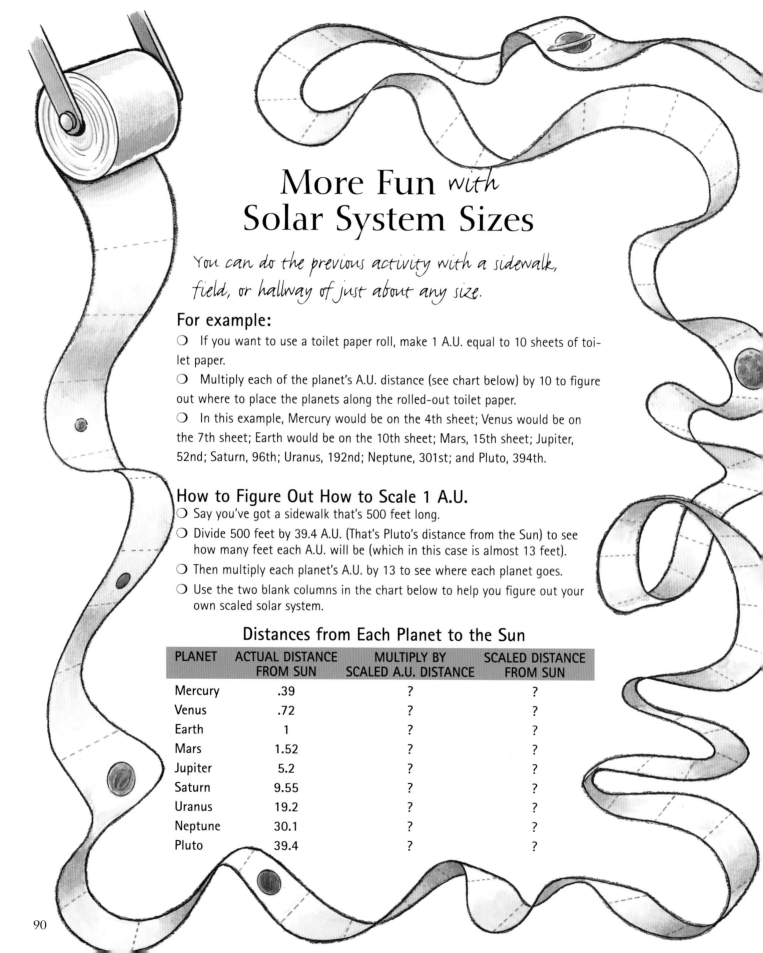

More Fun *with* Solar System Sizes

You can do the previous activity with a sidewalk, field, or hallway of just about any size.

For example:

❍ If you want to use a toilet paper roll, make 1 A.U. equal to 10 sheets of toilet paper.

❍ Multiply each of the planet's A.U. distance (see chart below) by 10 to figure out where to place the planets along the rolled-out toilet paper.

❍ In this example, Mercury would be on the 4th sheet; Venus would be on the 7th sheet; Earth would be on the 10th sheet; Mars, 15th sheet; Jupiter, 52nd; Saturn, 96th; Uranus, 192nd; Neptune, 301st; and Pluto, 394th.

How to Figure Out How to Scale 1 A.U.

❍ Say you've got a sidewalk that's 500 feet long.

❍ Divide 500 feet by 39.4 A.U. (That's Pluto's distance from the Sun) to see how many feet each A.U. will be (which in this case is almost 13 feet).

❍ Then multiply each planet's A.U. by 13 to see where each planet goes.

❍ Use the two blank columns in the chart below to help you figure out your own scaled solar system.

Distances from Each Planet to the Sun

PLANET	ACTUAL DISTANCE FROM SUN	MULTIPLY BY SCALED A.U. DISTANCE	SCALED DISTANCE FROM SUN
Mercury	.39	?	?
Venus	.72	?	?
Earth	1	?	?
Mars	1.52	?	?
Jupiter	5.2	?	?
Saturn	9.55	?	?
Uranus	19.2	?	?
Neptune	30.1	?	?
Pluto	39.4	?	?

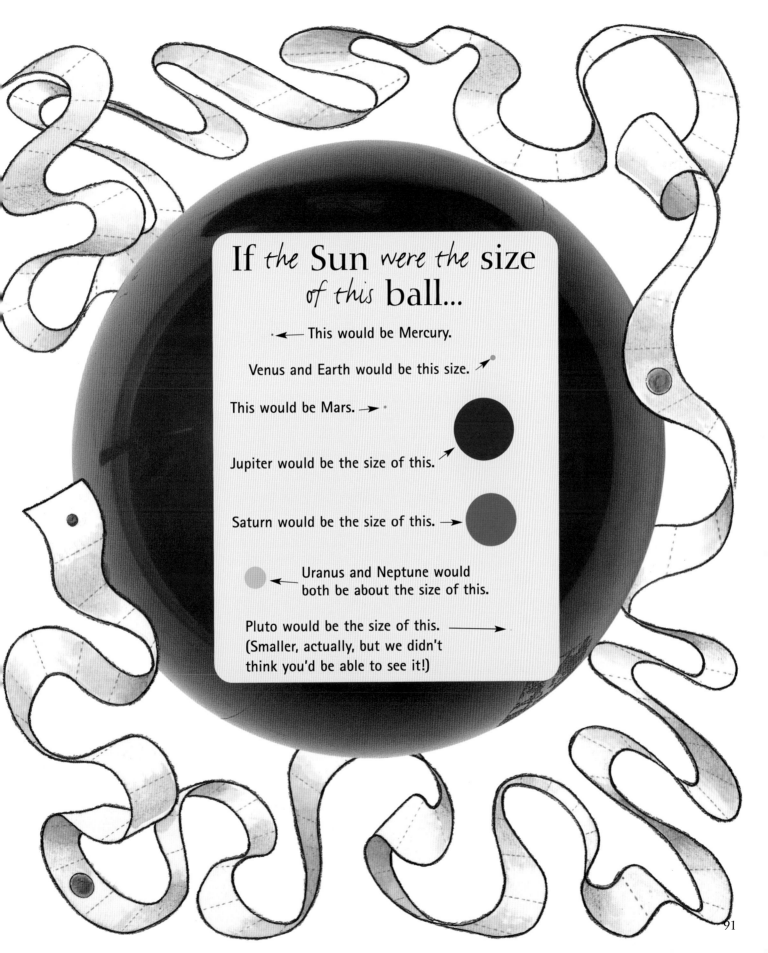

If the Sun were the size of this ball...

This would be Mercury.

Venus and Earth would be this size.

This would be Mars.

Jupiter would be the size of this.

Saturn would be the size of this.

Uranus and Neptune would both be about the size of this.

Pluto would be the size of this. (Smaller, actually, but we didn't think you'd be able to see it!)

Asteroids

An asteroid is made up of rock or metal (or a combination of both) and orbits the sun.

They're too small to be considered planets. Ceres, discovered in 1801, is the biggest asteroid, which is probably why it was seen first. It's 580 miles in diameter. The smallest ones are about the size of boulders.

Most of the asteroids in our solar system orbit between Mars and Jupiter. This is called the *asteroid belt*. Most asteroids are just hanging out there, crashing into each other and splintering into smaller bits. At rare moments, these asteroids will leave their orbit and crash into the planets.

One of the possible reasons dinosaurs went extinct is that a gigantic asteroid hit the Earth about 65 million years ago. The Chicxulub crater in Mexico may be the remnant of this impact. The crater is 110 miles wide—and people think that the asteroid was only 10 miles wide!

Asteroid Facts

○ Asteroids crash into things at 25,000 miles per hour (that's almost 7 miles a second!). This causes a lot of damage, even if they're relatively small.
○ In 1908, a very small asteroid hit the Earth in Siberia. It flattened 800 miles of forest.
○ Asteroids may be leftovers from the formation of the solar system.

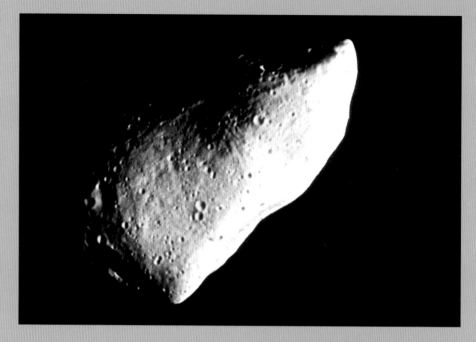

○ Some astronomers think that the asteroids in the asteroid belt were once a planet that got pulverized.
○ Some asteroids have their own small moons.
○ Scientists have discovered several hundred thousand asteroids. On average, dozens of new asteroids are discovered every month or two.

○ If you were navigating a spaceship through the asteroid belt, it really wouldn't be that hard (despite what all the movies might make you think). There's a lot of space in between the asteroids. If you were standing on an asteroid in the asteroid belt, you'd be lucky to see two asteroids anywhere near you.

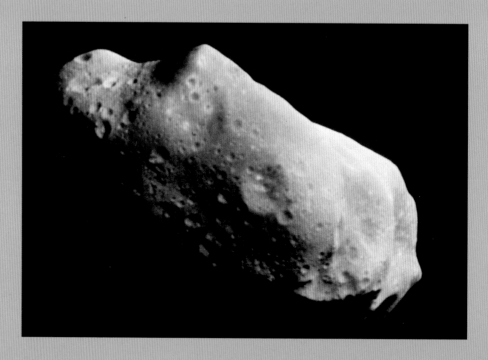

Dirty Snowballs *in* Space

Unlike asteroids, comets are made of ice, rock, and gas. Comets travel around the sun in oval-shaped paths. The time it takes can vary from several years to millions of years.

Where Do Comets Come From?

Some originate beyond the orbit of Pluto, while others come from a place called the Oort Cloud—a sphere of material that surrounds the solar system. There are also comets that live inside the solar system, such as Halley's Comet.

Parts of a Comet

Nucleus: The ice/rock center of the comet

Coma: The cloud of gases around the nucleus as the comet approaches the Sun

Ion Tail: Formed when the gases on the comet are blown by solar winds

Dust Tail: Formed when dust particles are pushed away by solar radiation (this tail can be millions of miles long)

How Comets Work

As a comet nears the Sun in its orbit, it begins to vaporize (the ice changes directly to gas). This produces a dust tail. As a comet approaches the Sun, its tail is following. When it moves away from the Sun, its tail leads the comet. This is due to the Sun's solar winds. Each time a comet passes close to the Sun, it loses more of its ice. Sooner or later, the comet will run out of material for its tails.

Halley's Comet orbits the Sun every 76 years. It won't pass Earth again until 2061.

Meteoroids

Meteoroids are objects too small to be asteroids.

Major Annual Meteor Showers

SHOWER NAME	ESTIMATED PEAK DATE
Quadrantids	January 3-4
Lyrids	April 21
Eta Aquarids	May 4-5
Delta Aquarids	July 28-29
Perseids	August 12
Orionids	October 21
Leonids	November 16
Geminids	December 13
Ursids	December 22

A *meteoroid* is a bit of rocky space debris. It can be the size of a grain of sugar, a pea, a baseball, or larger. These space rocks might be leftovers from when the solar system was cre-ated, bits broken off asteroids and planets, or the remains of a comet.

A *meteor* is the streak of light you see when the space rock enters Earth's atmosphere and burns up (maybe you've heard it called a shooting star).

If a meteor fragment survives the fiery journey through Earth's atmos-phere and lands on the surface, it's called a *meteorite*.

Meteorite Facts

○ Twelve or more meteorites crash-land on Earth every day.

○ Most splash into the ocean (remember, two-thirds of our planet's surface is water).

○ The odds of being hit by a mete-orite are 1 in 10 trillion.

○ Large meteorites can create craters

HOW DO SHOOTING STARS WORK?

There's no air in space, but when a meteor enters Earth's thick atmosphere 60 miles above the surface, it slams into air molecules while traveling as fast as 30,000 miles per hour. At that speed, air pressure and friction make the meteor glow white hot. We see it as a streak of light. At that point, most meteors deteriorate.

The best time to look for shooting stars (meteors) is usually between midnight and dawn. During a normal evening you may spot one or more meteors every 30 minutes or so.

On certain nights of the year Earth passes through bands of meteoroids left from passing comets, and a *meteor shower* happens. In some meteor showers you might see a meteor (or two) every minute. See the chart on page 94 for the dates of major meteor showers.

Note: The name of a meteor shower indicates in what star constellation you'll see the meteors appear in the sky.

just like those on the Moon and Mercury.

❍ About 30,000 years ago a meteorite smashed into what is now Arizona in the United States and blew out a crater 570 feet deep and 4,000 feet wide. You can visit it.

❍ If you picked up a meteorite immediately after it fell to the ground, it would be cold.

Spotting Satellites

There might be some nights when you spot something in the sky that doesn't move like a star or planet, seems too slow to be a shooting star, and is too small to be an airplane light. What's going on? It could be an alien spaceship, although more likely, it's one of the more than 10,000 man-made satellites that orbit Earth.

The best time to look for satellites is just after sunset or just before sunrise. That's when we're in darkness but satellites high in the sky are still reflecting sunlight. Once the satellites pass through Earth's shadow in the middle of the night, they can't be seen. By checking a recent astronomy magazine or website you can figure out when and where to find the International Space Station.

The Stars and Beyond

What Kind of Star Are You Made Of?

a) Rock star
b) Movie star
c) Ringo Starr
d) Supernova

Answer: All of the above, although everything in the Universe is made of very, very old stars called supernovas.

Stars contain all of the raw materials (like carbon and iron) that make up your body. When really big stars die, they spew out all of those raw materials, recycling them into other stars, nebulae, planets, black holes, and you.

Look up at the night sky. If you don't feel any sort of kinship, don't be disappointed. It's hard to keep in touch with family when the nearest relative—the star Proxima Centauri—is 23.6 trillion miles away. And all of the other stars in the sky are even farther away than that.

No wonder people have been fascinated by stars for so long. We've been using them to amuse ourselves at night (by making constellations), to navigate our way around the world, and more recently, to figure out what's going on in the Universe. The more we find out about stars, the more interesting they get.

Star Stats *and* Facts

○ Little stars are more common than big stars.

○ Sirius is the brightest star in the night sky. In 6,000 years it will be even brighter. It's slowly moving toward us.

○ Stars twinkle because their light gets distorted when it passes through the atmosphere.

○ Many stars don't hang out by themselves like our Sun does. About half of the stars in the Universe come in pairs (called *binary systems*).

○ Stars have surface temperatures that vary from 5,000 to 55,000°F.

○ You see different stars in the Northern and Southern Hemisphere.

○ When astronauts stood on the Moon, they couldn't see the stars very easily. In the same way that the full Moon makes it harder to see the stars from Earth, when the astronauts were on the Moon, the Earth was so bright it drowned out the stars.

○ The only star that isn't light-years away from us is the Sun. If the Sun were the size of the dot on this "i," the next star dot would be 10 miles away.

○ The brightest stars in the night sky have names. They are usually either Latin, Greek, or Arabic, depending on which culture's name stuck.

Way Far Away

What does it mean when something is light-years away? It means that it's so far away that it's hard for our minds to grasp just how far away it is. It's way far away.

Now, don't get confused by the word "year." A light-year is a measurement of distance, not time. It's how far light travels in one year. So, how far does light travel in one year?

5,900,000,000,000 miles (5.9 trillion miles).

Like we said, it's sort of difficult to imagine just how far away that is. Here's something that might help:

If you took how far light traveled in one second, which is 186,000 miles, how long would it take you to drive that distance (you'd need your driver's license and permission to drive your mom's car into space)? If you drove 60 miles an hour, it would take you nearly 130 days.

And how long would it take you to travel one light-year? Nearly 12 million years. You might have to drive a little faster than 60 miles per hour. Even if you could speed up to the speed of light (which you can't), it would take one year to get there. And it would take you four years to travel to our closest star neighbor, Proxima Centauri, which is four light-years away. That's 23.6 trillion miles.

Did You Know?

The farthest-away thing that you can see (without a good pair of binoculars or a telescope) is the Andromeda galaxy. It's two million light-years away. If the Andromeda galaxy disappeared tonight, you wouldn't know anything about it for two million years.

A Star Is Born

Stars are like people: they are born, live lives of fairly predictable lengths, and die.

What You Need

- ◯ Gas
- ◯ Dust
- ◯ Gravity
- ◯ Nebula (optional)
- ◯ Lots of time
- ◯ Sunglasses

What You Do

1. Stars are born in stellar nurseries called nebulae. If you want to make a star, first find a lot of gas and dust. It helps if the gas and dust are already in a nebula, but it's okay if they're all spread out across the Universe. (You'll just have to wait several billion years for gravity to pull it all into a nebula.)

2. Next, wait several million years while gravity pulls the gas and dust into a ball. Watch as the gas and dust get pulled even closer together by gravity. The pressure of the gas increases, which means more stuff is being stuffed into less space. The gas will start to get hot from the pressure.

3. Put on your sunglasses. When the core gets extremely hot, the nuclear reaction starts. The hydrogen atoms smash into each other, making helium. Your star will begin to shine.

4. Good job, you made a star. Now, how about lunch? (It won't take nearly as long to make.)

Now What?

◯ At this point, your star is an adult. It will continue to steadily burn its hydrogen for a very long time. (Our Sun is in this phase of life, and it will be about 5 billion years before the Sun uses up all of the hydrogen in its core.) These stars are called *dwarf* stars even if they're 10 times bigger than the Sun.

◯ In several billion years, when the star has used up all the hydrogen in its core, the star is near the end of its life. It will start to burn the helium in its core and the hydrogen near its surface. The star is getting ready to explode! Stars in this phase of life are called *red giants* because they swell up and get a lot bigger than they were. When this happens to the Sun, it will engulf the orbits of Mercury, Venus, Earth, and probably Mars.

◯ The size of the explosion depends on the size of the star. A medium-sized star, like our Sun, will make a medium-sized explosion, called a *nova*. When the star explodes, it flings off everything surrounding its core. After it explodes, the core slowly cools. It's called a *white dwarf*, because it's tiny and white hot. A white dwarf is so dense that a teaspoon of it would weigh 15 tons. And even though the name implies otherwise, a white dwarf can be any color after it cools—they all start out white hot, though.

◯ If a star is really big, it becomes a *supernova*. When the star explodes, it scatters debris all over. For a few days, this star might outshine its entire galaxy. Most of the star is blown into space. The debris from this will eventually become a nebula and give birth to new stars.

◯ The core of the star then shrinks to a *neutron star* or a *black hole*. (See page 120 for more about black holes.) A neutron star is even smaller than a white dwarf—but it weighs a lot more. A neutron star can be anywhere from 1 to 20 miles across, but a teaspoonful of neutron star would weigh a billion tons on Earth.

○ You can see the leftover remains of a supernova in the constellation Taurus. It's called the Crab Nebula because it looks like a crab on a black beach. The star that used to be there went supernova in 1054. Chinese astronomers recorded the event—it lasted 23 days and was four times brighter than Venus.

Stars Closest to Us

Star	Constellation	Distance (light-years)
Proxima Centauri	Centaurus	4.2
Alpha Centauri A	Centaurus	4.3
Alpha Centauri B	Centaurus	4.3
Barnard's Star	Ophiuchus	5.9
Wolf 359	Leo	7.6
Lalande 21185	Ursa Major	8.1
Sirius A	Canis Major	8.6
Sirius B	Canis Major	8.6
UV Ceti A	Cetus	8.9

How Does *the* Sun Measure Up?

If the Sun is the biggest thing you can see, and it's only a medium-sized star, just how big are those other stars?

What You Need
○ Scissors
○ Lots of string
○ A friend
○ Large cemented area
○ Sidewalk chalk
○ Tape measure
○ Calculator (optional)

What You Do

1. Cut a 3-inch length of string.
2. Have a friend hold one end of the string on the cement. Tape the other end of the string to a piece of chalk. With the string taut, draw a circle. (The circle will be 6 inches in diameter, since the length of string is the *radius*). Label this the Sun.
3. Consult the chart on page 103 for the size of the next star in solar diameters. To figure out how long you need to cut the next length of string, multiply the star's solar diameter by 3, the radius of the Sun model you just drew.

The number you get will be the radius of the star. For example, Castor A is 2 solar diameters. Multiply 3 inches (the radius of the Sun) by 2. Castor A should have a 6-inch radius. Cut another piece of string to 6 inches and use it to draw a circle. Castor A will be 12 inches in diameter, twice the size of the Sun.

4. Try step 3 with Aldebaran. Leave yourself a whole lot of room for this one. Do you even have enough string or chalk for Betelgeuse? How small is the string for a white dwarf star or a neutron star?

Aldebaran

Sun

Castor A

What Color
Is that Star?

Stars come in many different colors. The best time to see the different colors of the stars is in winter. (At night, of course.) Astronomers have figured out that the color of a star will tell us how hot it is.

Star Colors

Blue stars: 36,000 to 90,000°F
Blue-white stars: 18,000 to 36,000°F
White stars: 14,000 to 18,000°F
Yellow stars: 10,000 to 14,000°F (our Sun!)
Orange stars: 9,000°F
Red stars: 7,000°F

Star	Size
Sun	1 solar diameter
Castor A	2 solar diameters
Aldebaran	36 solar diameters
Rigel	50 solar diameters
Betelgeuse	550 solar diameters
A white dwarf	0.1 solar diameters

Arch to Arcturus

Big Dipper

Find Polaris

Polaris is the closest star to the north celestial pole—which means it's right above the north pole. It's been used for navigation for thousands of years. The ancient Greeks used it, and African Americans who fled slavery followed it to freedom.

What You Need
○ A dark, clear night

What You Do
1. Go outside and look up. Find the Big Dipper—it looks like a big rectangular bowl with a long handle (see

illustration). You should see seven stars forming what looks like a rectangular ladle.

2. To find the North Star, look at the two bright stars that form the front of the dipper's bowl. These are the pointer stars, and they are the farthest stars from the handle. Draw

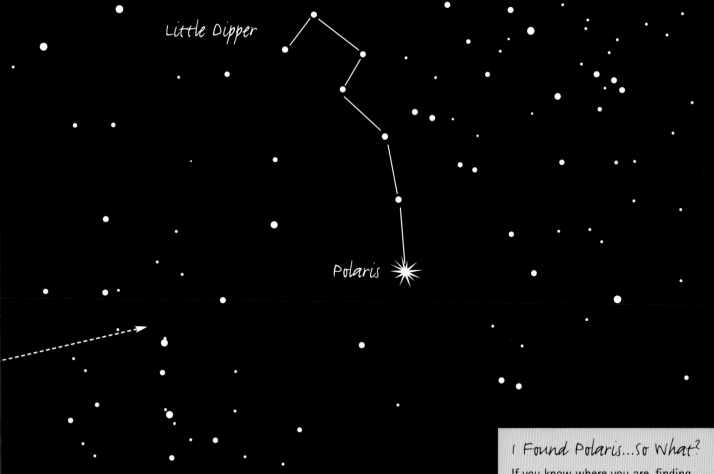

Little Dipper

Polaris

an imaginary line from these two stars that comes out of the bowl and goes in a straight line. Follow it until you come to a medium-bright star all by itself. That's Polaris.

3. If you're having trouble finding it, hold your fist out with your thumb and pinkie extended. Put your thumb over the pointer stars, pointing into the bowl. Your pinkie should line up with Polaris.

4. Once you've found Polaris, you've found the Little Dipper. (It looks like the Big Dipper,

but...smaller.) Polaris is at the tip of the Little Dipper's handle. The Big and Little Dippers are always positioned so that when one is right side up the other is upside down, with their handles facing in opposite directions.

5. The Big Dipper also points to another special star. If you follow the curve of its handle away from the bowl you'll come to Arcturus, a beautiful orange star that's 25 times bigger than our Sun and one of the brightest in the night sky.

I Found Polaris...So What?

If you know where you are, finding Polaris isn't going to be all that thrilling. But if you're lost, Polaris can be very, very helpful. It's called the North Star for a reason.

Face Polaris. Congratulations! You're facing north. Hold both of your arms out. Your left arm is pointing west. Your right arm is pointing east. Your back points south. Find a landmark in the direction you need to go and start walking toward it.

Polaris never sets and appears to not move, so it's always there for you. Unless you're in the Southern Hemisphere.

The astrolabe was invented nearly
2,000 years ago. Navigators used it to
help them find their latitude.
Latitude is a series of invisible made-
up lines that run around the Earth,
parallel to the equator. When you know
what your latitude is, you know something about where you are on Earth.

What You Need

○ Card stock (a heavy piece of paper, like an index card)
○ Ruler
○ Pen
○ Protractor
○ Scissors
○ String
○ Paper clip
○ Metal washer
○ Tape
○ Drinking straw

Latitude is a series of invisible lines that run around the Earth, parallel to the equator.

What You Do

1. Using the ruler, draw a line ¹/₂ inch down from the top of the card stock. Draw a second line ¹/₂ inch in from the right side of the card stock.

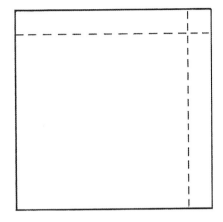

2. Put the protractor on the card stock. Line it up so that the line on the top of the card stock goes through the 90 degree mark on the protractor. Line up the ¹/₂-inch margin on the side with the 0 degree mark.

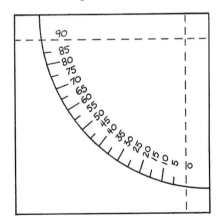

3. Transfer the angles on the protractor onto the card stock. For instance, draw a line for 5 degrees, 10 degrees, 15 degrees, etc. (If your protractor has marks only for every 10 degrees, mark these first, then put in the 5 degree marks halfway in between.) Write in the degree markings.

4. Trim the excess card stock away from the astrolabe. Don't cut off the ¹/₂-inch margins you made, though.

5. With the pen, punch a hole in the corner of your card stock. (That would be the one corner that is a right angle.)

6. Thread the string through the hole. Tie it to the paper clip to keep the thread attached to the astrolabe.

7. Pull the string down so that it hangs about 2 inches beyond the edge of the card stock.

8. Tie the washer onto the string.

9. Tape the drinking straw to the top edge of your protractor.

10. Hold the astrolabe up. The drinking straw should be on top and the other flat edge should be away from you. Look at the North Star through the straw. Then see where the washer is hanging. That measurement is your latitude. To find the altitude (height above the horizon) of any other star, find the star through the straw and look at where the washer is. Now you can tell your friends where to look for that star.

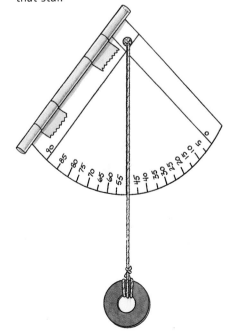

107

Star Light, Star Bright

The Greeks invented a scale for measuring the magnitude of stars more than 2,000 years ago.

The magnitude tells you how bright the star you're looking at is relative to other stars. The brightest stars in the sky had a magnitude of one. Stars that were just a little bit fainter than that were two, and so on.

After modern astronomers made more accurate observations of the brightness of the stars, they had to change the old scale. The very brightest stars don't fit on the scale anymore, so they're measured with negative numbers. Each magnitude is 2½ times brighter than the magnitude before it. You can see a magnitude 9 star with a good pair of binoculars, and a magnitude 12 star with a small telescope.

Variable Stars

The magnitude of a star can change over time. Astronomers call the stars that fluctuate *variable stars.* Sometimes a star will get brighter or dimmer because something within the star itself changes. There are stars that get bigger and smaller, and ones that have huge solar flares (kind of the like the ones the Sun has that make auroras, only much, much bigger). Binary stars appear to change magnitude when one star gets in front of the other.

Here are the five brightest stars we can see from Earth:

Sirius	-1.5 mag	8.7 light-years away
Canopus	-.7 mag	230 light-years away
Alpha Centauri	-.3 mag	4.3 light-years away
Arcturus	-.06 mag	38 light-years away
Vega	-.04	27 light-years away

If you lined up all of these stars at the same distance from Earth, which star would be the brightest? Canopus. Of all the bright stars, it's the farthest away. If it were at the same distance as the other stars, it would be really, really, really bright.

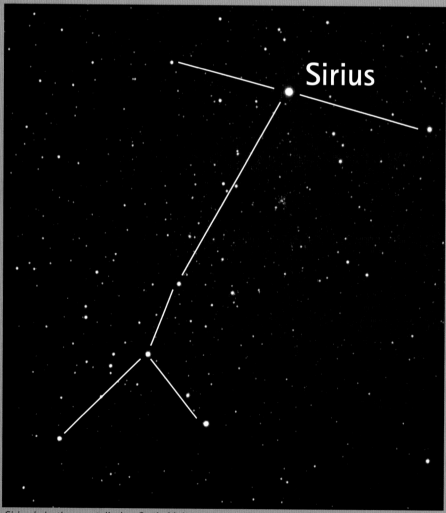

Sirius

Sirius is in the constellation Canis Major.

Catching Some Rays

Electromagnetic (that's EM for short) radiation is just a fancy name for light.

Radio Waves

Microwaves

Infrared

Optical

Your eyes can only see one kind of EM radiation—called visible light. But the Universe makes a whole lot more than that, and scientists rely on many forms of EM radiation to get a better picture of the Universe.

The forms of EM radiation are called radio waves, microwaves, infrared, optical, ultraviolet, x-rays, and gamma rays. All EM radiation is made up of vibrating waves of electric and magnetic fields, and they all travel at the speed of light (186,000 miles per second).

Radio Waves

You've listened to your radio a lot, but did you know that many objects in space (ranging from planets such as Jupiter to the cores of galaxies) broadcast radio waves? Radio waves also tell scientists about how gases are spread out in our galaxy.

Microwaves

You can use these to study the Universe to communicate with satellites, or to cook your popcorn. The left over radiation from the Big Bang shows up as microwave radiation.

Infrared

Infrared waves tell us about molecules in space. Nebulae show up best as radio and infrared rays. Stars that are obscured within dark nebulae can be seen more easily in the infrared part of the spectrum.

Optical

Optical radiation is light that our eye can see, including all the colors of the rainbow. Hotter objects, such as stars, emit most of their energy at optical and ultraviolet wavelengths.

Ultraviolet

Ultraviolet light is mostly blocked out by the Earth's atmosphere, but enough of it gets through to cause skin cancer, so wear that sunblock! Ultraviolet light can tell us about the temperatures, densities, and composition of interstellar gas.

X-Rays

Very active stars and the machine at the doctor's office produce x-rays. Newly formed stars often produce X-rays, giving away their youthful status.

Gamma Rays

Gamma rays (and X-rays) provide scientists with information about pulsars, neutron stars, black holes, and active galaxies. Astronomers have observed sources of gamma rays in the sky of unknown origin. These "gamma ray bursts" are short-lived but may occur in all parts of the sky.

Ultraviolet

X-rays

Gamma Rays

Constellations

Stars—they're sparkly, bright, and absolutely free entertainment! It's no wonder people have been looking at them for a very long time.

Many cultures have invented their own unique *constellations*. A constellation is a group of stars that people have made pictures out of. Most of them are animals or mythological characters. There are 88 official constellations (mostly made up by the Babylonians and Greeks more than 2,500 years ago), and they aren't all in the sky at once. As the Earth orbits the Sun, you can see different constellations.

If you're on the equator, you can view all the constellations in a year. If you are on the north or south pole, you'll be able to see only the part of the sky that lies directly above you. That means you'll get a great view of Polaris or the south celestial pole, but you'll never see the other half of the sky.

The constellations are still out during the day, but you can't see them because the Sun is too bright. You have to look at them after sunset or before sunrise.

Did You Know?

The Big Dipper isn't a constellation. It's officially known as an *asterism*, which is a group of stars that forms a pattern in the sky but is NOT one of the 88 recognized constellations. The Big Dipper is part of the constellation Ursa Major.

Consult a sky chart to find out when and where to locate these and other constellations

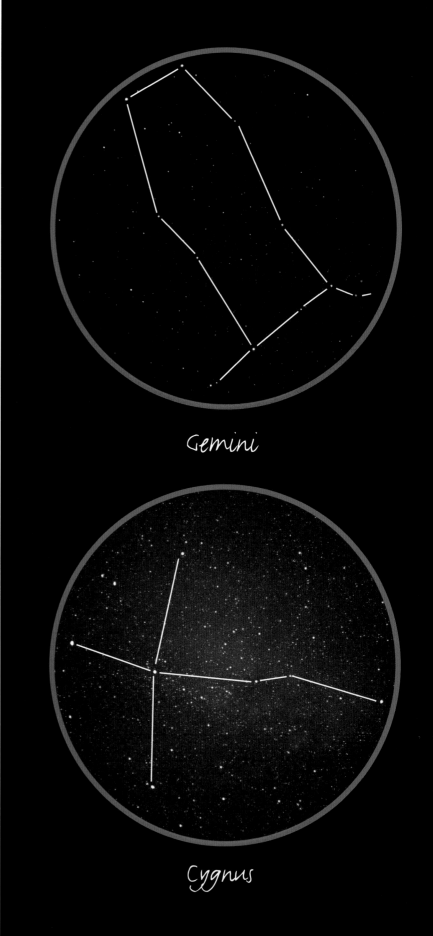

Gemini

Cygnus

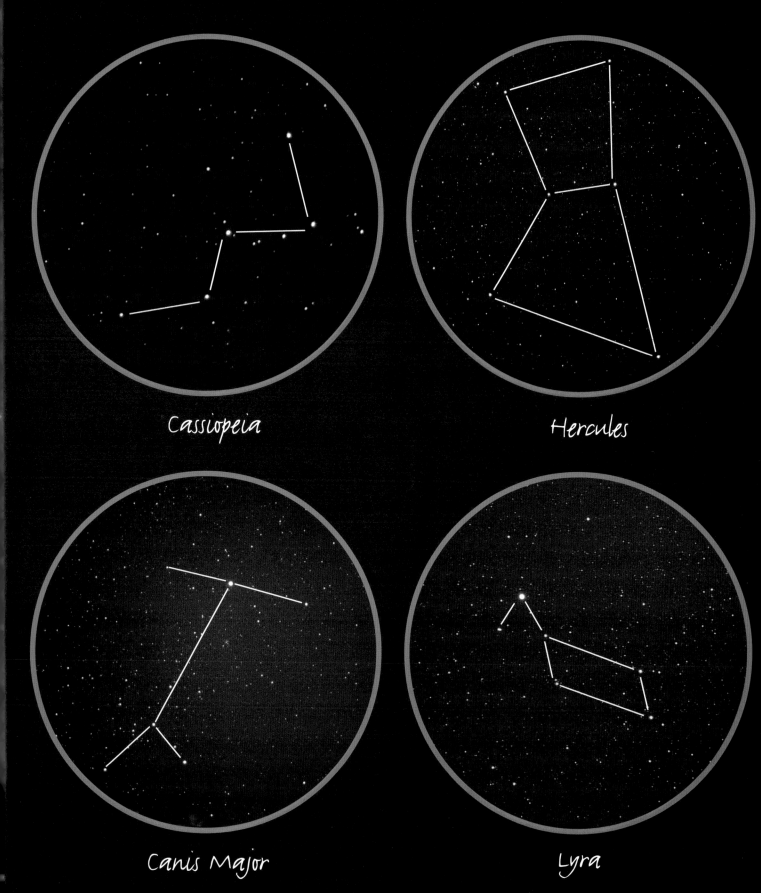

Cassiopeia

Hercules

Canis Major

Lyra

Constellation *in a* Can

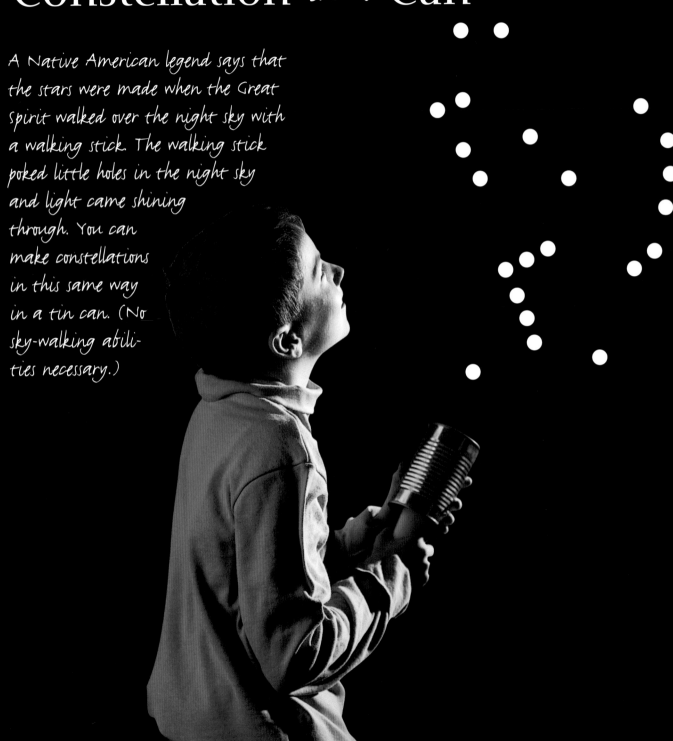

A Native American legend says that the stars were made when the Great Spirit walked over the night sky with a walking stick. The walking stick poked little holes in the night sky and light came shining through. You can make constellations in this same way in a tin can. (No sky-walking abilities necessary.)

What You Need

○ Tin can
○ Tracing paper
○ Pencil
○ Scissors
○ Tape
○ Small nail
○ Hammer
○ Flashlight

What You Do

1. Put your clean tin can upside down in front of you.

2. Trace the pattern of one of the constellations shown below onto a piece of the tracing paper. Flip the paper upside down and tape it to the bottom of the can. (If you don't flip the paper over, your constellation will be backward.)

3. With the hammer and nail, punch holes where the stars are located.

4. Take off the tracing paper, and look through the can. Do you see the constellation?

5. You can shine a flashlight through the can to project the constellation onto your wall or ceiling.

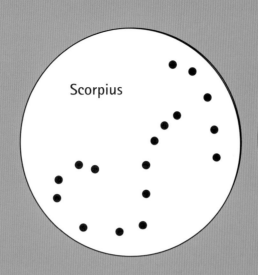

Scorpius

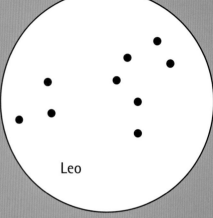

Leo

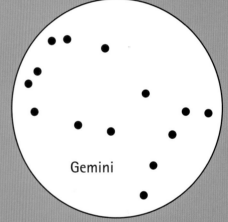

Gemini

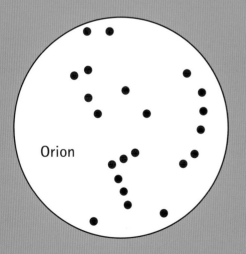

Orion

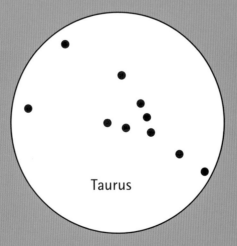

Taurus

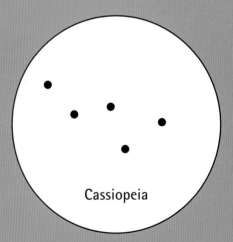

Cassiopeia

The Three-D Constellation

If your spaceship got lost orbiting Alpha Centauri, you wouldn't be able to find the Big Dipper and follow it home. Why?

The constellations look like themselves only when you're standing on Earth. The stars that make up the constellations are all at different distances from us. They line up in different ways depending on where you are standing. Take a look at Orion with this activity.

In ancient Greek mythology, Orion was the greatest hunter ever.

Betelgeuse

Bellatrix

Mintaka

Alnilam

Alnitak

Saiph

Rigel

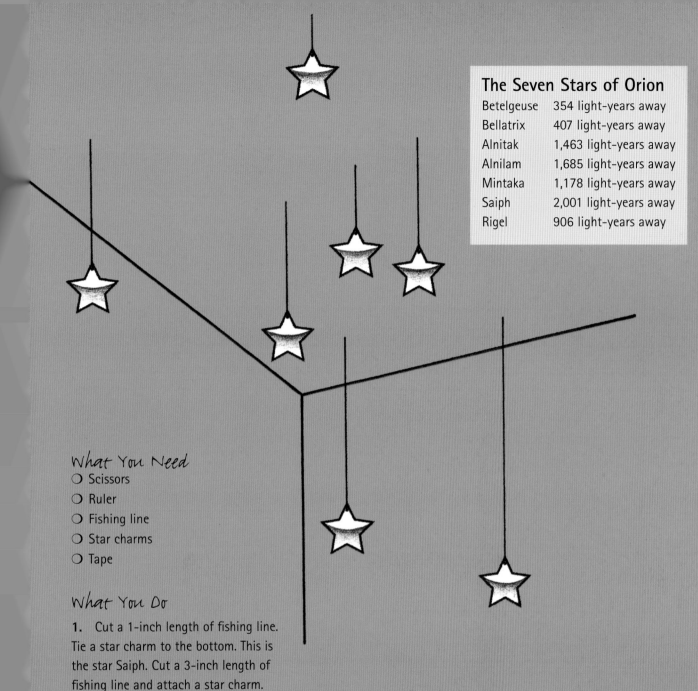

The Seven Stars of Orion

Betelgeuse	354 light-years away
Bellatrix	407 light-years away
Alnitak	1,463 light-years away
Alnilam	1,685 light-years away
Mintaka	1,178 light-years away
Saiph	2,001 light-years away
Rigel	906 light-years away

What You Need

○ Scissors
○ Ruler
○ Fishing line
○ Star charms
○ Tape

What You Do

1. Cut a 1-inch length of fishing line. Tie a star charm to the bottom. This is the star Saiph. Cut a 3-inch length of fishing line and attach a star charm. This is Alnilam. Cut a 3^1/$_2$-inch length of monofilament and attach a star charm. This is Alnitak. Cut a 5-inch length of fishing line and attach a star charm. This is Mintaka. Cut a 6-inch length of fishing line and attach a star charm. This is Rigel. Cut a 9-inch length of fishing line and attach a star charm. This is Bellatrix. Cut a 10-inch length of fishing line and attach a star charm. This is Betelgeuse.

2. Use the diagram on page 114 to tape the stars to the ceiling where they belong.

After you finish hanging Orion, look at it from several different angles. At which angle does it look like Orion? Can you make other constellations with the stars when you look at it from different angles?

Stories in the Stars

When the first stargazers looked up at the night sky, they tried
to make sense of it by finding patterns in the stars.

Our ancient Greek, Sumerian, and Arabic ancestors saw in the stars the animals, people, and gods that affected them, and used the star patterns to visually tell the stories that explained their world. These pictures have become our constellations. But other cultures had their own stories that the constellations represented. Here are several myths from around the world that explain the Big Dipper (part of the constellation Ursa Major).

○ The Iroquois Indians who lived in the northeastern United States thought the Big Dipper was a bear, but they saw only the rectangle of the dipper as the bear. The three bright stars in the handle are three hunters chasing the bear. The first hunter carries a spear to kill the bear.

The middle hunter carries a pot to cook the bear in once they catch it. The pot is the faint companion star of Mizar, Alcor. The last star is the final hunter, who is gathering wood to cook the bear.

○ The Cherokee Indians who lived in the southeastern United States saw the Big Dipper as a canoe full of lacrosse players. When their canoe runs into the horizon, all the players hop out and play lacrosse all night long. Then they get back in the canoe and wait for the next game.

○ To the Siberians, the Big Dipper was an elk that carried the Sun in its antlers.

○ The Germans thought that the Big Dipper was a big wagon.

○ The Britons saw King Arthur's chariot.

○ In the Middle East, the stars of the dipper formed a coffin for a man who was killed by the North Star. The stars in the handle of the dipper are the man's three sons. They want to avenge their father's death, so they constantly circle the North Star, waiting for their opportunity.

Make up your own constellation and the story behind it. Then see if you can get a friend to find the same constellation.

Galaxies: Where *the* Stars Hang Out

A galaxy is a massive, gigantic collection of stars. On average, there are 100 billion stars in a galaxy. Some are bigger, and some are smaller.

An Elliptical Galaxy

We live in the Milky Way galaxy. Astronomers think there are about 200 billion stars in our galaxy. If you could count two numbers a second, it would take you 3,000 years to reach 200 billion—and you'd be really hungry and tired by the time you finished. (Not to mention old!) Every star you can see with your naked eye at night is part of our galaxy.

Galaxies come in three different shapes: spiral, elliptical, and irregular.

❍ Spiral galaxies look like flattened disks. They have long arms that spiral out from the center. Their centers tend to be slightly rounder and thicker than their edges. Spiral galaxies contain some old stars and a lot of young stars. They also give birth to a lot of new stars. The Milky Way galaxy is a spiral galaxy. You can see one of the arms of the Milky Way in the night sky.

❍ Elliptical galaxies look like big globs in the night sky. They don't have a lot of young stars in them. Most of their stars are old and dying.

❍ Every other kind of galaxy is an irregular galaxy. Astronomers think they got all bent out of shape when other, larger galaxies passed close by. Irregular galaxies don't have any particular shape.

A Spiral Galaxy

The Yellow Galaxy

Galaxy Stats and Facts

○ The closest large galaxy is M31, or the Andromeda galaxy. You can see it in the summer in the constellation Andromeda. It's 200 million light-years away.

○ All of the galaxies in the Universe are still moving away from each other as the Universe expands.

○ The farther away a galaxy is, the faster it is moving away from us.

○ The Sun is 27,000 light-years away from the center of the Milky Way.

○ If you look at Sagittarius you're looking toward the center of our galaxy.

○ It takes the Sun 225 million years to complete one revolution around the center of the Milky Way.

○ The Milky Way is 100,000 light-years across.

○ Most galaxies are found in small groupings or large clusters. Our cluster is a small family of galaxies known as the Local Group. The nearest cluster can be seen within the constellation Virgo.

○ The Milky Way is slowly eating one or two tiny satellite galaxies right now! You have to be in the Southern Hemisphere to see it, though. It's a thin trail of luminescent debris called the Magellanic Stream.

○ The most distant galaxies known are found on the very edge of the Universe. These galaxies are called "blue fuzzies" because that's what they look like from here. They're so far away we know nothing about them.

The Andromeda Galaxy

The Milky Way

The term "Milky Way" means three different things: the galaxy we live in, a soft band of light you can see in the night sky, and the candy bar you just ate.

The soft band of light that is called the Milky Way is one of the spiral arms of our galaxy. Here's how you can see it.

What You Need

○ A clear, dark night
○ An out-of-town location
○ New Moon or third quarter in the winter or summer

What You Do

1. Light pollution often obscures the Milky Way from view. If you can, get out of town.
2. Look for the start of the Milky Way in the northwest or northeast corner of the sky. It will look like a narrow band of lit-up clouds that runs all the way to the southwest or southeast corner of the sky. Until Galileo and his telescope, people had no idea the Milky Way was full of stars. Just about everybody who looked at it before saw it as a path or a road through the sky.

The Milky Way with Halley's Comet

Black Holes

Black holes are one of the most mysterious things in the Universe. You can't see one—not even with a powerful telescope.

Black holes suck up everything around them—light, planets, X rays, radio waves, everything. That's one of the reasons they're so mysterious. Black holes are found by looking at how they affect the stuff we *can* see—which is the stuff that's getting sucked in. Some scientists believe that once something gets sucked into a black hole, it leaves the Universe and goes somewhere where the physical and natural laws of the Universe are not obeyed. No wonder black holes are a science fiction staple.

More on Black Holes

❍ Most black holes (and there aren't a lot of them) are leftover star explosions. On average, a star 10 times the size of our Sun will compress into a black hole that's 37 miles across.

❍ There are even bigger black holes that exist at the center of galaxies. Scientists think they're not the remains of stars, but they have no idea what made them. There is evidence of a supermassive black hole in the center of the Milky Way. It's called Sagittarius A*, and it has as much mass as 2 or 3 *million* Suns.

How It All Began: The Big Bang

Twelve billion years ago, there was NOTHING.
No planets, no stars, no Earth, no light, no nothing.

Then...something happened. In one moment there was an incredibly dense, unbelievably tiny speck filled with light. A trillion-trillion-trillionths of a second later, the Universe expanded outward from that single point. Did it make a big bang? Well, no, but that's what the theory of how the Universe was formed is called. It's not over, either. The Universe is still expanding. How? Take a look.

What You Need

- ○ Balloon
- ○ Marker
- ○ Tape measure
- ○ Paper and pencil
- ○ Paper clip
- ○ String

What You Do

1. Draw some different galaxies on the balloon with the marker. Remember, they don't all have to be spirals. Measure the distances between the galaxies and record them on your paper.

2. Blow some air into the balloon. Fill it until it's about the size of your fist. Put the paper clip over the end of the balloon to keep the air in. Measure the spaces between the galaxies with the string. Then measure the length of the string on the tape measure and record it.

3. Take off the paper clip and continue to inflate the balloon, stopping at intervals to take more measurements. Look at how far the galaxies have moved away from each other as the balloon (representing the Universe) expanded. This is still happening right now. Don't overinflate the balloon! If it explodes, it will make a big bang, but this is in no way related to the REAL Big Bang.

Galactic Address

If you had a nice conversation with an alien from a planet near Vega and she decided to come visit you, could you tell her where you live? To entertain guests from a galaxy far, far away (or even this one) you'll need to know what your galactic address is.

Fill in the blanks:
Your name:
Street address:
City:
State:
Country:
Hemisphere (circle two): North, South, East, West
Solar system: Planet Earth, third planet from the Sun
Spiral arm: Outer edge of the major spiral arm, two-thirds of the way out from the center
Galaxy: Milky Way
Local galaxy cluster: The Local Group

Now address your envelope and send it. The only problem is figuring out how many stamps to put on it!

Anybody Out There?

There are trillions and trillions of stars and billions and billions of galaxies.

With all that stuff out there, it seems sort of surprising that so far, we've found only one planet that supports life. That's us. Are there aliens out there? And if so, why can't we find them? It would help if we could travel through space faster than we can. Distances between stars are so great that it would take thousands and thousands of years to get to our nearest neighbors.

So, until we figure out how to travel at least the speed of light, what can we do? In 1977, two space probes were launched by NASA. Known as Voyager 1 and 2, these probes are currently heading toward the outer boundaries of the solar system. They have enough power to operate at least until 2020, and by that time they will be more than 10 billion miles away from Earth. Eventually, they will pass other stars. In some 296,000 years, Voyager 2 will pass Sirius. The Voyagers are destined—perhaps eternally—to wander the Milky Way. With that in mind, scientists didn't simply include computers and data-receiving machines on the Voyagers. They also included information about Earth and its people, including a message carried by a 12-inch copper record (the kind your parents and grandparents listened to—no CDs yet!) containing sounds and images selected to portray the diversity of life and culture on Earth. They also added musical selections from different cultures and eras, and spoken greetings from Earth people in 55 languages.

Hey, we may not be able to travel to the stars yet, but maybe somebody out there can. And perhaps they will find one of our Voyager calling cards and get in touch. How cool would that be?

Glossary

Altazimuth mount: A mechanism that allows both horizontal and vertical motion of the telescope.

Altitude: The angle of a celestial object above the horizon.

Aperture: The opening in a telescope or other optical instrument that determines the amount of light that passes into it.

Aphelion: The point in a celestial body's orbit where it's farthest from the Sun.

Asterism: A group of stars that forms a pattern in the sky but is not one of the 88 recognized constellations. It is usually a part of a constellation.

Asteroid: A small celestial, rocky body that orbits around the Sun.

Astrolabe: An instrument that measures the altitude of celestial objects.

Astronomy: The study of objects in outer space.

Atmosphere: The gases surrounding a planet retained by its gravitational pull.

Aurora: Glowing streaks of color in the night sky caused by charged solar particles colliding with air molecules in the upper layers of the Earth's atmosphere near the poles.

Big Bang: The theory that the Universe was created when it suddenly expanded out of the violent explosion of an incredibly dense and hot but miniscule speck filled with light.

Binary star: A system of two stars that orbits around a common center.

Binoculars: An optical instrument with two small telescopes that allows distance viewing.

Black hole: The void left over after a star explodes, and its core collapses under it own tremendous gravity. Everything nearby, even light itself, is sucked in.

Blue fuzzies: Extremely distant galaxies that formed when the universe was much younger.

Bore sight: To align the viewfinder with the main telescope.

Catadioptric telescope: One that uses both reflective and refractive optical devices.

Celestial body: Any large object in outer space.

Ceres: The first asteroid discovered, and the largest, with a diameter of 581 miles.

Chromosphere: The thick layer of gas just above the Sun's surface.

Comet: A celestial object composed of ice and rocky material that has a very elliptical orbit around the Sun, resulting in an elongated vapor tail when it reaches the inner solar system.

Conjunction: When planets group together in a small part of the sky.

Constellation: A formation of stars imagined to resemble a design.

Corona: A luminous ring surrounding a celestial body; the Sun's thin, faint, outermost layer.

Crater: A hole usually caused by an impact from a comet or asteroid.

Crescent: The shape the Moon appears before its first and after its last quarter, curved with pointy tips.

Differential rotation: When the poles of a spinning celestial body take a different amount of time than the equator to make a full rotation.

Dwarf: The longest stage in a star's evolution. Later stages result in an increase in the size and the amount of light produced.

Earthshine: Light reflecting from the Earth onto the shadow of the Moon's disk.

Eclipse: When one celestial body covers up another as viewed from a particular vantage point.

Elliptical: Having the shape of an ellipse.

Ellipse: A slightly flattened circle.

Equatorial mount: A mechanism that allows a telescope to spin along an axis that is parallel to the Earth's rotation.

Equinox: Occurs twice a year when the day and the night are of equal lengths of time.

Eyepiece: The lens closest to the eye.

Far side: The side of the Moon that we never see from Earth.

Galaxy: A group of billions of stars all orbiting a common center.

Gibbous: When the Moon is more than half, but less than fully lit.

Gravity: A force of attraction exerted by one body upon another.

Horizon: The horizontal line where the ground meets with the sky.

Jovian planet: A giant, rapidly-rotating, low-density sphere of gas with no solid surface, located in the outer part of our solar system.

Latitude: Imaginary lines that run from East to West that are parallel to the equator.

Magnitude: A measure of the amount of brightness of a star.

Mass: The amount of matter (or stuff) that is contained within something.

Meridian: An imaginary North-South line across the sky, which celestial objects cross when they reach their highest position in the sky.

Meteor: The streak of light created by a meteoroid entering the Earth's atmosphere and burning up.

Meteorite: A meteoroid fragment that has survived the fiery journey through Earth's atmosphere and landed on the planet.

Meteoroid: A bit of rocky space debris smaller than an asteroid.

Meteor shower: A number of meteors that appear together in the sky and seem to come from the same place, usually because the Earth is passing through a debris field.

Milky Way: The galaxy to which our solar system, the Sun and all other stars we see in the night sky belong.

Moon: A smaller celestial body that orbits a planet.

Near side: The side of the Moon that we always see from Earth.

Nebula: A collection of gas and dust where stars are born.

Neutron star: A very dense core left over from a massive star that has exploded and collapsed. Usually only directly detectable by the X-rays it gives off.

Nova: The explosion from a medium-sized or smaller star.

Objective lens: The first lens to receive light rays and form the image in an optical instrument.

Orbit: To revolve around a celestial body.

Path of totality: The area over which the darkest part of the Moon's shadow passes along the Earth during a total solar eclipse.

Penumbra: The lighter part of an eclipse's shadow.

Perihelion: The point in a planet's orbit where it is closest to the Sun.

Photosphere: The surface of the Sun or a star.

Planet: A non-luminous celestial object larger than an asteroid or comet which revolves around a star.

Planetoid: A planet-sized asteroid.

Radius: A line from the center of a circle to its edge.

Red giant: A star near the end of its life that has swollen much larger than its original size.

Reflector: A telescope in which light is collected and focused by a concave mirror.

Refractor: A telescope in which light is collected and focused by lenses.

Regolith: The surface layer of lunar soil.

Retrograde motion: An illusion caused by overtaking an object, in which although its speed has remained constant, it appears to slow down, move backward, and then forward again.

Rotation: The act of turning on an axis.

Satellite: A celestial body or human constructed object that orbits a planet.

Seismometer: An instrument that measures the strength of earthquakes or impact tremors.

Solstice: When the Sun reaches its most northern and southern position in the sky, resulting in the longest day of the year (first day of summer) and the shortest day of the year (first day of winter).

Star: A self-luminous celestial body, visible at night as a stationary, twinkling point of light.

Sundial: An instrument that tells solar time by casting the Sun's shadow on a calibrated dial.

Sunspots: Cooler regions in the outer layers of the Sun which look like small, dark spots.

Supernova: The violent explosion of a massive star larger than the Sun.

Telescope: An optical instrument that uses lenses, mirrors, or both to permit observation of distant objects.

Terminator: A line that divides the lit and shaded areas of a moon's or a planet's disk.

Terrestrial planet: A small, rocky, and dense planet, located in the inner part of our solar system.

Tidally locked: When a celestial object turns on its axis at exactly the same rate that it orbits around another body.

Umbra: The dark portion of an eclipse's shadow.

Universe: The Earth, the planets, stars, galaxies, and anything else that is present in space, including all matter and energy.

Variable star: A star that changes in its brightness and dimness over time.

Waning: A stage when the area of illumination on an object is decreasing.

Waxing: A stage when the area of illumination on an object is increasing.

White dwarf: The tiny, dense, white-hot core that remains after a star has died and exploded.

Zenith: The point directly above an observer, or the highest point above the observer's horizon.

Zodiac: The path that the Sun, Moon and planets take when they move through celestial sphere, divided into 12 parts, each named after a constellation.

Online Resources

The Moon
http://tycho.unso.navy.mil/vphase.html
View the phase of the Moon for any date and time, from the 1800s all the way to the year 2199.

http://www.moon-phases.com/
Two complete photographic maps of the Moon and pictures of the Moon in different phases. Test your knowledge of the Moon and its phases by taking one of the quizzes from this website.

http://www.galaxies.com/Info/Applets/moon.htm
This website uses animation and graphics to show each day of the phase and the four main phases of the Moon.

http://www.netaxs.com/~mhmyers/moon.tn.html
Is there really a man in the Moon? What about the lady in the Moon? What is a blue Moon? This website explains many myths about the Moon and has cool Moon photos.

http://www.solarviews.com/cap/moon/vmoon1.htm
Is there really a dark side of the Moon? Check out this website for images of the far side of the Moon.

http://www.moon-phases.com/moon-pictures/pictures.html
What's it like on the Moon? Check out the Alpine Valley, the Apennine Mountains, and a variety of craters on the Moon's surface.

http://www.moon-phases.com/photographic-map/moon.html
If you love maps this is the website for you! Just click on the Moon to get a photographic map of that section.

http://www.mreclipse.com/LEphoto/LEgallery1.html
Lunar eclipses are solid proof that the Earth is round. Check out some cool photos of lunar eclipses.

http://www.netaxs.com/~mhmyers/cdjpgs/last4.jpg
More pictures of lunar eclipses.

The Sun
http://solar-center.stanford.edu/folklore/folklore.html
The Sun has different meanings to different cultures and their people. This website contains numerous mythological stories about the creation of the Sun.

http://directory.google.com/Top/Science/Astronomy/Observatatories/
This website contains a list of links to solar observatories around the world.

http://www.lpl.arizona.edu/~rhill/alpo/solstuff/recobs.html
An excellent site with more than 100 solar observations from around the world. The A.L.P.O. site also contains rotational charts of solar activity, as well as a solar animation page.

http://www.solarviews.com/eng/sun.htm
Check out photographs of Sun spots, solar flares, and eclipses.

http://www.lmsal.com/YPOP/Spotlight/Tour/index.html
Pack your bags for an amazing online tour. Your destination is the Sun! This website is packed full of cool interactive graphics and information about the brightest light in our sky. Questions explored on this tour include everything from the color of the Sun to what it's like on the inside. This website also includes some of the stranger facts about the Sun.

http://www.astro.uva.nl/demo/sun/
Take a 20 minute journey of the Sun on this website. In the "Trip Through the Sun" you will observe solar flares larger than 10 Earths and solar winds of up to 1,000 mph. This site contains time lapse movies of the Sun's photosphere along with other fascinating facts and photographs.

http://www.northern-lights.no/
View one of nature's most beautiful phenomena—The Aurora Borealis, or Northern Lights. Learn how aurora are created and where the best places are to see them.

http://www.worldtime.org/cgi-bin/wt.cgi
A cool website for seeing where the Sun's shadow lies across the Earth.

http://aa.usno.navy.mil/data/docs/RS_OneYear.html
This page provides a table for any location worldwide of the times of sunrise and sunset, moonrise and moonset, and the beginning and end of twilight for one year.

http://solar-center.stanford.edu/activities.html
Tour this website to find exciting activities, images, interactive tools, and a variety of other resources to learn about the Sun.

The Solar System
http://www.materialworlds.com/sims/SolarSystem/worksheetPlanetOrbits.html
Check out the simulated tracking of the entire solar system and view the paths taken by the planets around the Sun. Use the simulation program on this website to answer questions about the shape, speed, and direction of the planets.

http://www.dustbunny.com/afk/planets/planets.htm
Take a journey through our solar system. You can visit all the members of our planetary family, discovering fascinating facts about each one, by clicking on the names of the planets.

http://www.dustbunny.com/afk/sky/sky.htm
See a guide for finding the planets each month of the year on this site.

http://www.dustbunny.com/afk/howdo/findplanet/findplanet.htm
Visit this website to find out how scientists find other planets.

http://zebu.uoregon.edu/~js/ast121/lectures/lec08.html
This website contains charts and pictures of planet atmospheres and magnetic fields.

http://library.thinkquest.org/C002416/venus/
This website offers general information about Venus. It contains photographs and probe observations.

http://atsrosun.tn.cornell.edu/courses/a102/lectures/Lecture
This website offers a series of lecture panels on Venus. The discussions answer questions like, "Why is it so hot?" "What's in the atmosphere?" There is also a summary of spacecraft missions.

http://www.math.rice.edu/~ddonovan/Lessons/eratos.html
Did you know that Alexandria Eratosthenes' discovered the diameter of the Earth by peering into a well? For some interesting details about his discovery, and how to determine the diameter of the Earth for yourself, visit this website.

http://antwrp.gsfc.nasa.gov/apod/ap001127.html
Click here to see a night view of the Earth from space.

http://www.windows.ucar.edu/tour/link=pluto/pluto_orbit.html
Visit this website for great images and information on how Pluto goes in and out of being the furthest planet from the Sun.

Stars
http://stardate.org/resources/gallery/gallery_detail.php?id=268
If you enjoy watching the stars, check out these links to star charts, constellations, and star lore.

http://stardate.org/resources/gallery/gallery.php/Category=7000
A great starting point for young astronomers. Learn about a vanishing planet, the super giant star Eta Carinae, and the Milky Way.

Comets
http://amazingspace,stsci.edu/resources/explorations/comets/lesson/facts/Fact6/index_nf.html#top
A great site for famous comets and when you can see them.

Other Fun Sites
http://spaceflight.nasa.gov/realdata/sightings/Ssapplications/Post/SightingData/sighting_index.html
A cool link to figure out when and where the International Space Station or one of the space shuttles are located.

http://www.marsacademy.com/traj/traj7.htm
When is the best time to leave Earth to get to Mars? When is the best time to get back home? This website explains the importance of launch windows for shuttles and rockets exiting and entering the Earth's atmosphere.

http://www2.crl.go.jp/hk/slr/whatis/whatis.html
An interesting site about satellite laser ranging (SLR) and how these SLR stations are able to determine the Earth's rotation, orbits of satellites, and plate tectonic motion of our planet.

http://almagest.as.utexas.edu/~rlr/mlrs.html
So what are those satellites looking at? Check out this website for great pictures and information about the University of Texas McDonald Observatory and its scientific pursuits.

http://www.phys.uconn.edu/~mcdonald/ph155/sidereal.html
How is a sidereal day different from a solar day? The answer to this question and more about solar time can be found on this website.

Photography Credits

The photos on pages 9, 18,19, 20, 21, 32, 34, 37, 38, 45, 62, 73, 106, 108, 110-111, and 114 appear courtesy of Robert D. Miller.

The photos on pages 12-13, 22, 28, 29, 35, 68-69, 71, 78, 79, 80, 83, 92, and 96-97 appear courtesy of NASA.

The photo on page 116 appears courtesy of the NAOA.

The photos on pages 1, 2-3, 7, 10, 11, 24-25, 31, 32, 37, 43, 46, 47, 48-49, 50, 62, 63, 64, 67, 68-69, 70, 74, 75, 76, 77, 78, 79, 80, 81, 84, 85, 86, 93, 94-95, 95, 98, 99, 101, 102-103, 116, 117, 118, 119, 120, 122, and 123 appear courtesy of Getty Images.

The alien on page 123 appears courtesy of Corbis.

The photos of telescopes on pages 26 and 27 appear courtesy of Celestron. Much thanks to Jennifer Adams.

Acknowledgments

ASTRONOMICAL THANKS TO:

The stellar kids who modeled for us:
Emily Auman, Saschwa Auman, Jake Hill,
Isaac Paul, Lacey Pelly, Daniel Pinelli, Noah
Ratner, Kayleigh Rhatigan, Moriah Rullmoss,
Phillip Treadway

Greg Doppmann for sharing the magnitude
of his enthusiasm for astronomy, his knowl-
edge, and his time.
Celia Naranjo for once again making the
impossible possible.
Shannon Yokeley for making sure nothing
important fell into a black hole.
Robert D. Miller for the awesome pictures
and on-the-fly astronomy lessons.
Orrin Lundgren for turning nebulous instruc-
tions into cool illustrations.
Steve Mann for taking phenomenal pictures.
Jeanée Ledoux for making sure we spelled
words like regolith and altazimuth correctly.
Leslie Huntley for making the projects.
Tana Jencks for helping us find our models.

And the usual cast of characters at Lark
Books (especially Deborah Morgenthal, Dawn
Cusick, Veronika Gunter, Delores Gosnell,
Rosemary Kast, Jeff Hamilton, Chris
Winebrenner and Nathalie Mornu) for keep-
ing us in orbit.

Metric Conversions

½ inch = 1.3 cm
1 inch = 2.5 cm
2 inches = 5 cm
3 inches = 7.6 cm
4 inches = 10.2 cm
5 inches = 12.7 cm
6 inches = 15.2 cm
7 inches = 17.8 cm
8 inches = 20.3 cm
9 inches = 22.9 cm
10 inches = 25.4 cm
11 inches = 27.9 cm
12 inches = 30.5 cm

To convert inches to centimeters,
multiply by 2.54.
To convert feet to centimeters,
multiply by 30.
To convert yards to meters, multiply by 0.9.
To convert miles to kilometers,
multiply by 1.6.
To convert pounds to kilograms,
multiply by 0.454.
To convert tons to metric tons,
multiply by 0.9.
To convert Fahrenheit to Celsius,
subtract 32 and then multiply by 0.56.

Index